Doctrine
Made Flesh

I0181824

Doctrine Made Flesh

Faith and the Grammar of Love

under the supervision of
K. Steve McCormick

Theological Essentials

©Digital Theological Library 2025
Library of Congress Cataloging-in-Publication Data

K. Steve McCormick (creator).
Doctrine Made Flesh: Faith and the Grammar of Love/ K. Steve
McCormick
135 + xvi pp. cm. 12.7 x 20.32
ISBN 979-8-89731-972-5 (Print)
ISBN 979-8-89731-184-2 (Ebook)
ISBN 979-8-89731-292-4 (Kindle)
ISBN 979-8-89731-216-0 (Abridged Audio Discussion)
            1 Theology — Doctrinal
            2 Faith — Christianity
            3. Love — Religious aspects — Christianity
BT750 .M36 2025

This book is available in other languages at
www.DTLPress.com

Cover Image: "The New Creation" was created by K. Steve McCormick,
using AI

In Gratitude

I give thanks for the energy of God's infinite vulnerable love that has kept me walking the path that begins in God and is ever returning home to God.

I am unspeakably grateful for the Spirit's tether, my vision of loveliness, Tricia, my soul mate and best friend. Her love has been like the gentle kiss of butterflies, softening my gaze and attuning my heart. Her voice has been like the song of hummingbirds released in the garden with every beat of their wings; she has gifted me with a melody of grace, fierce and fragile, faithful and free.

She has kept my feet on the ground when my voice soared into fire. She has saved this truth-teller more than once from the wounds of those who feared what they could not see. Her love steadies me still.

And to my students, past and future, who have taught me more than I could ever teach: thank you for showing me the face of God in your questions, your wonder, your courage, and your hope. You are the song of New Creation taking flesh.

Contents

Series Preface

Artificial Intelligence (AI) is changing everything, including theological scholarship and education. This series, *Theological Essentials*, is designed to bring the creative potential of AI to the field of theological education. In the traditional model, a scholar with both mastery of the scholarly discourse and a record of successful classroom teaching would spend several months — or even several years — writing, revising and rewriting an introductory text which would then be transferred to a publisher who also invested months or years in production processes. Even though the end product was typically quite predictable, this slow and expensive process caused the prices of textbooks to balloon. As a result, students in developed nations paid more than they should have for the books and students in developing nations typically had no access to these (cost-prohibitive) textbooks until they appeared as discards and donations decades later. In previous generations, the need for quality assurance — in the form of content generation, expert review, copy-editing and printing time — may have made this slow, expensive and exclusionary approach inevitable. However, AI is changing everything.

This series is very different; it is created by AI. The cover of each volume identifies the work as "created under the supervision of" an expert in the field. However, that person is not an author in the traditional sense. The creator of each volume has been trained by the DTL staff in the use of AI and *the creator has used AI to create, edit, revise and recreate the text that you see*. With that creation process clearly identified, let me explain the goals of this series.

Our Goals:

Credibility: Although AI has made — and continues to make — huge strides over the last few years, no unsupervised AI can create a truly reliable or fully credible college or seminary level text. The limitations of AI generated content sometimes originates from the limitations of the content itself (the training set may be inadequate), but more often, user dissatisfaction with AI-generated content arises from human errors associated with poor prompt engineering. The DTL Press has sought to overcome both of these problems by hiring established scholars with widely recognized expertise to create books within their areas of expertise and by training those scholars and experts in AI prompt engineering. To be clear, the scholar whose name appears on the cover of this work has created this volume — generating, reading, regenerating, rereading and revising the work. Even though the work was generated (in varying degrees) by AI, the names of our scholarly creators appear on the cover as a guarantee that the content is equally credible with any introductory work which that scholar/creator would pen using the traditional model.

Stability: AI is generative, meaning that the response to each prompt is uniquely generated for that specific request. No two AI-generated responses are precisely the same. The inevitable variability of AI responses presents a significant pedagogical challenge for professors and students who wish to begin their discussions and analysis on the basis of a shared set of ideas. Educational institutions need stable texts in order to prevent pedagogical chaos. These books provide that stable text from which to teach, discuss and engage ideas.

Affordability: The DTL Press is committed to the idea that affordability should not be a barrier to knowledge. *All persons are equally deserving of the right to know and to understand.* Therefore, ebook versions of all DTL Press books are available from the DTL libraries without charge, and available as print books for a nominal fee. Our scholar/creators are to be thanked for their willingness to forego traditional royalty arrangements. (Our creators are compensated for their generative work, but they do not receive royalties in the traditional sense.)

Accessibility: The DTL Press would like to make high quality, low cost introductory textbooks available to everyone, everywhere in the world. The books in this series are immediately made available in multiple languages. The DTL Press will create translations in other languages upon request. Translations are, of course, generated by AI.

Our Acknowledged Limitations:

Some readers are undoubtedly thinking, "but AI can only produce derivative scholarship; AI can't create original, innovative scholarship." That criticism is, of course, largely accurate. AI is largely limited to aggregating, organizing and repackaging pre-existing ideas (although sometimes in ways that can be used to accelerate and refine the production of original scholarship). Still while acknowledging this inherent limitation of AI, the DTL Press would offer two comments: (1) Introductory texts are seldom meant to be truly ground breaking in their originality and (2) the DTL Press has other series dedicated to publishing original scholarship with traditional authorship.

Our Invitation:

The DTL Press would like to fundamentally reshape academic publishing in the theological world to make scholarship more accessible and more affordable in two ways. First, we would like to generate introductory texts in all areas of theological discourse, so that no one is ever forced to "buy a textbook" in any language. It is our vision for professors anywhere to be able to use one book, two books or an entire set of books in this series as the *introductory* textbooks for their classes. Second, we would also like to publish traditionally authored scholarly monographs for Open Access (free) distribution for an advanced scholarly readership.

Finally, the DTL Press is non-confessional and will publish works in any area of religious studies. Traditionally authored books are peer-reviewed; AI-generated introductory book creation is open to anyone with the required expertise to supervise content generation in that area of discourse. If you share the DTL Press's commitment to credibility, affordability and accessibility, contact us about changing the world of theological publishing by contributing to this series or a more traditionally authored series.

With high expectations,
Thomas E. Phillips
DTL Press Executive Director
www.thedtl.org
www.DTLpress.com

Author's Preface

The *Parabola* of Love
Interpreting the Icon of Doctrine Made Flesh

The cover of this book is more than design; it is a vision. Drawn from the title *Doctrine Made Flesh: Faith and the Grammar of Love*, the image offers a theological icon, a visible sign of the invisible grace of God animating this entire work. It is a visual homily shaped by the metaphor of St. Irenaeus's "two hands of God," Christ and the Spirit, guiding us on the long, luminous journey from the Creator and back to the Creator. This is the journey of faith. It is the way of love. It is the path of creation and new creation braided into the same arc of divine desire.

At the center of the image is the Christ, the Word made flesh, in whom all things hold together. Through the Spirit, "She Who Is," the Breath of Life, this same Word that once spoke the cosmos into being now takes on flesh, becoming the second incarnation of God. Creation was the first incarnation: the Word going forth in love, forming the world through wisdom ingrained in the grain of the universe. The Spirit hovered, breathed, called, and still breathes, binding all things in love. Through the "two hands of God," creation came to be and through them, it is being gathered again toward its home in God.

The Colossian hymn (1:15, 20) sings the mystery at the heart of this icon: that all things, visible and invisible, material and spiritual, have been created through Christ and for Christ. That in Christ, all things hold together. That in the blood of the cross, God is reconciling everything to himself. Following this icon, is the tree of life that is always planted along this path, rooted in soil yet transfigured by glory. Even the small signs of evolutionary delight, like the rare non-binary cardinal nestled in the garden, whisper the truth that God's future knows no boundary, no exclusion, no fixed dichotomy. All are swept into the ever-widening dance and song of New Creation.

This is a book about faith, not faith reduced to creedal assent, but faith as trust in the One who is infinitely trustworthy. It is a book about doctrine, not as ecclesial control, but as the grammar of God's love that is shaped by the Spirit who breathed creation into existence and raised Christ from the grave. It is about the Church, not as an institution, but as the living breathing epiphany of God's love, called to embody the good news for all creation that the world is returning home to the God who first spoke it into being.

This vision echoes the ancient witness of Irenaeus, whose theology of creation and New Creation lies at the heart of this book. Against the Gnostic impulse to divorce Creator from creation, he bears witness to their unbreakable union, one not merely willed but woven into being itself. This is no contractual bond, but an ontological communion: God is infinite love, eternally vulnerable, ever giving. Creation, from its first breath, pulses with the delight of the Creator's love, each creature trembling with the memory and promise of divine joy. There is no path to God that bypasses creation, for it is here, in soil and song, breath and body, that the Creator's love dwells. Through the wisdom and energy of that love, creation is being gathered, healed, and transfigured. God's future and the future of all that is are not parallel but braided, drawn forward together in the Spirit's patient labor toward New Creation. The beginning is entrusted to the end, and the end is already alive in the beginning. This is the grammar of love, the language of faith that flows with the grain of the universe, for the infinite, vulnerable love of God is never absent, always nearer than breath, ever drawing all things toward their radiant fulfillment in Christ.

The Paradox of Love's Return

Here lies the paradox: that the infinite vulnerable love of God, when flung into the cosmos, does not diminish by dispersal but expands in sweep, in reach, and in gathering power and in creative emergence. What is cast outward from the heart of God is not merely sent "only" to return, it is sent to create and to gather as it goes. Because what is thrown out is infinite vulnerable love, it draws everything it touches, every created thing already belonging to the Creator, into its widening arc. The return is not repetition but consummation. The whole creation is being swept up in the loving return, not just echoing the origin but fulfilling the Creator's promise: the promise of New Creation. This is not a closed circuit or a finished script, but an open *parabola*, expanding, gathering, and glorifying, and co-creating as it returns, carrying all things home to the One who first flung them forth in vulnerable trust.

And in that return, something even more astonishing occurs: the first delight of the Creator over creation, sung in joy and spoken in love, is not simply remembered but magnified beyond measure. For everything that has been gathered back has not only belonged to the Creator but has participated in the joy, glory, and the creative freedom of divine love. What is flung out in infinite vulnerable trust returns bearing the gift of creation's own response, faith, praise, wonder, and communion, yes, but also its creative expansion of infinite love itself. Here, the paradox deepens: infinite love, by nature without boundary, is also infinitely vulnerable, open to surprise, risk, and transformation not only in relation to creation, but within God's own life. Not merely in how God engages us, but in how God's very being, Infinite Vulnerable Love, is always stretching, opening, responding, and expanding in communion with the creation God loves. This is not a compromise of divine nature; it is its fullest expression. For the One who flung infinite love into finite space has irrevocably bound Godself to all that is, such that what is returned from creation not only magnifies creation but participates in the ongoing becoming of God's joy and love. This is the mystery of infinite vulnerable love: God's being knows no bounds and the interminable vulnerable trust that is God's love proves it. This is not contradiction, but mystery. A holy impossibility made possible by the One whose nature is to love without reserve and to trust without limit.

To follow Christ is to trust as Christ trusted the Spirit. To live by faith is to participate in the very faith of Christ, a faith that is nothing less than love's full surrender to the

Creator's promise. The Spirit who filled Christ now fills us. The energy of that same love, the breath that birthed galaxies and stirred the garden and raised Christ from the grave, is what sings in our souls.

So go into the world. Make music with your friends. Let your friendships stretch the *parabola* of God's immense love. Let the fireflies of your imagination delight the Creator. Watch as the Spirit tethers you to fellow travelers, some unexpected, some even formerly called enemies. Let your heart be attuned to the wisdom that thrums in every quark and corner of creation. It is all drenched in the joy and glory and love of God.

This book is one small attempt to say what faith feels like when it is full of the Spirit's breath, shaped by Christ's love, and fixed on God's future. It is an offering as a labor of love, a theological doxology, to help the Church remember the grammar of love, and to recover a faith alive with the energy of first things.

Follow the sweeping path of the *parabola*, and you will find yourself in the ever-widening path of God's love, thrown out in trust, returning in glory, and always exceeding itself in the wild wideness of the infinite vulnerable love that is God from everlasting to everlasting. Nothing is left behind.

May it be.

Introduction
Speaking Love as Faith's First Word

"Come, Holy Spirit, and kindle in us the fire of your love.
Take our minds and think through them.
Take our lips and speak through them.
Now, take our souls and set them on fire."
Amen.
Ancient Christian Prayer

Speaking Love
Doctrine as Faith's First Word

This ancient prayer of the Church captures the heart of this book. Doctrine is not merely the Church's intellectual response to divine truth, it is the Church's faithful grammar of God's love, spoken from a heart ignited by the Spirit and shaped in prayerful communion. What follows is not abstract speculation, but the Church's effort to articulate this love with clarity, reverence, and hope, spoken from a heart ignited by the Spirit and shaped in prayerful communion with the living God. What is doctrine, if not the Church's way of speaking about the God it has come to know through grace and love through prayer? And what is faith, if not the Spirit's gift, a trust awakened in the soul by the love of God, breathed into life through prayer and worship?

This book arises from the conviction that Christian doctrine is not a museum of frozen statements, nor a relic preserved behind the glass of ecclesial certainty, but a living, breathing witness formed through prayer, tested in suffering, and expressed in love. Doctrine, at its best, is the faithful grammar of God's love, language shaped by the Spirit to express, embody, and enact that love in communal life, witness, and hope because it is the Church's way of breathing with the Spirit, confessing, remembering, and proclaiming the God who is Love.

This book offers a theological invitation, a call to inhabit doctrine not as a theory to master, but as a shared language of belonging shaped by divine love and prayerful encounter. It invites readers, especially students, ministers, and pilgrims of faith, to see doctrine not as a closed system of abstract theological propositions, but as the Church's living grammar, life giving breath shaped by the Spirit. Doctrine is not the enemy of experience or imagination. Nor is it a relic of a rigid past. It is love remembered, sung, embodied, and shared. Since doctrine breathes and lives in the respiration of the Spirit to speak with the grammar of divine love, the aim is not simply to understand formalized doctrine, but to be transformed by it. To that end, since faith filled with the energy of God's love is received in prayer, this book is best read prayerfully. May it lead you to deeper wonder, deeper courage, and deeper love.

We live in an age of deep disorientation. The fractures of our time, social, political, ecological, spiritual, cry out for a Church that knows not only what it believes, but how to live that belief with joy, humility, and power. In such a moment, recovering doctrine as the Church's faithful grammar of divine love becomes not only a theological task but a pastoral necessity, inviting communities to speak, pray, and live the truth of God's love amid the dissonance of our age. Faithful doctrine matters because it forms communities capable of such faithful witness and costly love. It helps us pray deeply, lament truthfully, and love generously, and wait together in hope for the world to come.

This work explores the vital relationship between faith and doctrine, through a Wesleyan lens, grounded in the "first principles" of the Gospel. This exploration is both theological and devotional, historical and contemporary. It affirms that faith is born in prayer by the Spirit, and that doctrine emerges as the grammar of that Spirit-awakened love. Creeds, dogmas, and theological formulations arise, not first from institutional ambition or the need for control, but from communities who have encountered the living God in prayer, Scripture, worship, and shared life. Scripture and sacrament, suffering and song, memory and mission all converge to form a living vision of doctrine made flesh. Yet when these first principles are lost, when the grammar of love is replaced by a language of institutional power, doctrine becomes a tool of prescription rather than a witness to transformation. The truth of the Gospel sets us free, but when doctrine is untethered to the Spirit who teaches us to pray and reduced to an ecclesial checklist of creeds and doctrinal affirmations severed from the love of Christ, it no longer speaks the language of faith or faithfulness.

This dynamism of love is not rootless. Rather than a mere method of theological reasoning, the Wesleyan quadrilateral, Scripture, tradition, reason, and experience, functions as a Spirit-shaped grammar of grace. It enables doctrine to remain both grounded and generative, echoing the movement of divine love in ever-new contexts. Wesleyan theology offers a uniquely compelling model for doctrinal development using, Scripture, tradition, reason, and experience, as the means of grace to reach our end in God.

This quadrilateral does not reduce doctrine to static formulations but allows it to remain means of grace that are faithful to the Gospel while responsive to new contexts. Rooted in grace and shaped by the Spirit, Wesleyan theology models how doctrine can remain both grounded and generative, both ancient and adaptive. Doctrine remains grounded in the Scriptures, the worshiping life of the Church, and the ongoing guidance of the Spirit, the Spirit who continues to animate and enlarge our faithful understanding and vision of God's promise of New Creation. And here, Wesleyan theology offers something essential: a faithful yet flexible model of doctrinal development, rooted in Scripture, tradition, reason, and experience, all under the providential care of God's love.

In contrast to glaring visions of doctrine as frozen or permanently fixed formula, I affirm a living, breathing tradition, one that breathes deeply with the Spirit, who is the Lord and Giver of life. Doctrine is dynamic because the Church's faith is dynamic, ever breathing with the Spirit, pulsing with divine love, and adapting to the rhythm of God's ongoing work in the world. Creeds are not cages of faith but songs, composed by communities attuned to the Spirit's leading through the means of grace. Dogma, at its best, does not silence questions but holds space for holy mystery. The Vincentian Canon, "everywhere, always, and by all" must not be used to prematurely eclipse the eschatological hope of New Creation. The doctrines of the Church continue to expand and stretch with the grammar of God's infinite and vulnerable love because the future of God and all creation awaits the Spirit's fulfillment of Christ's promise "to make all things new."

Much of my academic work has centered on the development of the Church's doctrine. Along the way, I have discovered deep wells of wisdom and grace within the Church's theological tradition. But everything changed the moment I came to see that these teachings, creeds, dogmas, doctrines, were not forged in abstract speculation but born in prayer. That realization forever transformed the way I view the doctrinal life of the Church.

For nearly forty years, I have taught the beauty, truth, and grace of the Church's faith. I have sought, however imperfectly, to live into it, to embody what I have taught. And yet, I have always found myself something of a prophet on the inside edge of the Church's tradition, looking outward to the margins of society and culture, held fast by a "faith filled with the energy of God's love." From that vantage point, I have watched with grief and deep sorrow as institutional Christianity, in many forms and across many communions, has begun to reverse the living order of the Gospel. Increasingly, belonging has come to depend upon intellectual assent to doctrine, creedal affirmation required before communion, before relationship, before grace. In many places, a kind of creedal and doctrinal certainty has taken hold, replacing the Spirit-born faith that is the true heart of the Church. Clearly, this is not the Gospel.

The Good News is that we already belong, to God, to one another, to the reconciling love of God in Christ through the power of the Spirit. We believe because we have been awakened in prayer, because we have been kindled by the Spirit, because the fire of divine love has stirred our hearts to trust. Doctrine, then, is not the entryway into the Church, but the Church's response to the God who has already drawn near. Good doctrine is the faithful articulation of our shared belonging in light of God's love.

And yet, too often, as soon as the Creed is formed, the Church moves from confession to consolidation, from communal doxology to institutional regulation: such as in the aftermath of the Council of Nicaea, when Nicene orthodoxy was wielded to marginalize dissenting voices and suppress theological diversity, it becomes a tool of control. Doctrine, once a doxology, hardens into dogma used to divide. This book, then, is both a recovery of faith and doctrine and a plea, for a renewal of the Church's witness through a Spirit-breathed grammar of love, that doctrine might once again function as the faithful grammar of divine belonging rather than a boundary of exclusion. It is a work of deep ecumenical hope, a labor offered in service to the unity for which Christ prayed in his great high priestly prayer. It is a call to remember that the Spirit still breathes, that faithful doctrine can still sing, and that the love of God remains the Church's first and final word, a love that sends us into the world not with fear or control, but with open hands and hearts, longing for a Church renewed in compassion, communion, and the courageous hope of New Creation.

The First Order of Knowing
Love Before Language

This book seeks to recover what might be called the "first order of knowing," a form of knowledge not born of human construction, but born of the infinite, vulnerable love of the Creator. From the beginning of creation to its promised fulfillment, God speaks the Word and suffuses heaven and earth with divine glory. This way of knowing is predicated on, and continually dependent upon, the Creator speaking, not only into what we see and hear, but into what we know and how we know. As such, doctrine may be understood as a "second order" response: the Church's faithful articulation of this divine initiative, a grammar shaped by the first order of God's loving self-disclosure. This framing understands doctrine as the grammar of divine love, language born from the Creator's initiating love, sustained by the Spirit, and expressed faithfully by the Church.

This first order of knowing unfolds as mystery and mercy:

- The Word who spoke creation into existence is the Love that is God.
- The Word who became flesh is the Love that is God.
- The Word who breathed with the flame of Love at Pentecost is the Spirit who formed the Church as the living, breathing Body of Christ, a communion of diverse voices bound together by grace, speaking in many tongues with a shared grammar of divine love.
- The Word who promises New Creation is the Love that is God, our beginning and our future end.

This Love that is God is the source of faith. Flowing from this divine initiative, faith awakens in the soul and finds expression through prayer and doctrine, forming the Church's responsive grammar of love.

Faith as Gift
Awakened by the Spirit, Not Earned

Faith is not our achievement. It is God's gift, radically different from a works-based righteousness or intellectual assent. Unlike faith framed as merit or as a rational conclusion, this gift emerges from grace alone, calling us into humble trust and relational intimacy with God. It is not something we possess, but something God gives. It does not arise from intellectual persuasion or personal striving, but from the Spirit's awakening, an unearned trust that flows from divine initiative. This divine initiative invites the Church into a posture of doctrinal humility, reminding us that all theological language is secondary, always a response to God's first Word of love.

Faith emerges not from within the self, but from encounter. It is the gentle yet unshakable assurance that we are known, seen, and loved by God. It is the Spirit's loving whisper, calling us by name before we ever speak a word.

Prayer and the Breath
The Spirit's Grammar of Trust

Faith is born in prayer and love, but even prayer is not first a human act. Prayer is the Spirit's own breathing within the heart, igniting awe, surrender, and trust, and shaping the communal life of the Church through shared rhythms of adoration, confession, hope and awe, surrender, and trust before any creed is confessed or word is spoken. The Church does not invent faith through theological articulation; it receives faith through Spirit-given adoration.

John Wesley asked repeatedly with pastoral urgency: "Is your faith filled with the energy of God's love?" For Wesley, this love is never sentimental or abstract. It is catholic love, Triune love poured out from the Father, revealed in the Son, and poured into our hearts through the Holy Spirit. This divine love is not a doctrine to be defined, but a fire to be caught.

Charles Wesley captures this vision in his hymn:
O Love Divine, how sweet thou art!
When shall I find my willing heart
All taken up by thee?

This is not a call for doctrinal precision, it is a plea for the living God to inhabit the heart, forming in us an embodied grammar of love that transcends mere words.

Love Before Belief

Love precedes belief. Adoration precedes articulation. We are drawn into faith; we do not reason our way to it. Faith is not constructed by human logic or by the willful choice to believe, it is breathed into being by divine love. As the Apostle Paul writes, "God's love has been poured into our hearts through the Holy Spirit who has been given to us" (Rom 5:5). For the Wesley's, this outpouring is nothing less than the indwelling of the whole Trinity.

Faith may be born in the heart, but it is nurtured in the Body, the Church, Christ's living breathing body, where shared practices, communal worship, and mutual love give rise to doctrine not as private conviction but as a common language shaped by grace. John Wesley insisted: "There is no holiness but social holiness." The Christian life could not be sustained in isolation. The Church is the school of love, the habitat of grace, the dwelling where believers are shaped into the likeness of Christ through word, table, and daily life.

The Word Before Words
Listening to the Creation God Loves

Before the Church ever spoke its creeds, the Word was already speaking. The Word through whom all things were made has never been silent. Creation itself is the first sacrament of the Creator's making: the mountains and rivers, the beasts and the trees, the sun and the stars, all give voice to the Creator's glory, without human words. As the psalmist says, "Day to day pours forth speech, and night to night declares knowledge" (Ps 19:2).

Creation speaks a grammar older than theology, a doxology that predates doctrine. Doctrine does not replace creation's witness; it responds to it. It is the Church's faithful attempt to listen, to name, and to echo what has already been declared from the beginning: that God is Love. In this way, the eternal speech of the Word becomes the grounding impulse behind the Church's task of doctrinal articulation, not to define mystery, but to participate in its praise and proclaim its presence. Think of it!

It is the discipline of waiting, without grasping, for the Word to speak. From this posture, doctrine cannot be control or conquest. It must be spacious and reverent. It must arise from wonder, and never as certainty. Doctrine is the faithful grammar of God's love. It arises from reverent attention to a world already speaking God's name. It is not the invention of the Church, but her humble response.

Doctrine and creed emerge not to replace this "first order of knowing," but to give shape to how we know in love, to help the Church remember and confess what she has received. The creeds were never meant to enclose mystery in formulas, but to protect the Church's witness to the love of God revealed in Christ, a love already singing in creation, already breathing in prayer.

Historically, doctrine has followed the movement of faith. The Church did not begin by defining Christ, it began by worshiping him. The earliest Christians were caught up in the Spirit's life long before they had words to describe it. Doctrine came later, not to constrain that life, but to bear faithful witness to it. The task of doctrine is to weave the grammar of God's love into our imagination and hope of God's beloved Kin-Dom on earth as it is in heaven.

So, we return to the heart of this book's central claim: doctrine is the faithful grammar of God's love, language born from love, shaped by love, and returning us to love. It is a way of speaking that arises from love, serves love, and leads back to love. It does not silence the mystery but invites us to dwell within it. It does not begin with words, but with the Word who became flesh, and with the creation that still bears the glorious presence of its Creator. Doctrine becomes flesh to learn the faithful grammar of God's love and carry all things toward the New Creation.

This book is offered as one small echo of that love, seeking to learn and speak the grammar of love made flesh, the very theme of Doctrine made Flesh. My prayer is that we may faithfully learn to speak it, together.

Chapter One
From Communion to Creed

To profess the Christian faith is to be drawn into the language of the Spirit, a language shaped by the Word, nourished in worship, and ordered toward love.
Rowan Williams
"God is love, and those who abide in love abide in God, and God abides in them." (1 John 4:16)

The Church Believes Because It Belongs

Before the Church had a creed, it had a meal. Before doctrine was written, bread was broken, a meal that seeded the grammar of love which doctrine would later give voice to. The first Christians gathered not to debate propositions, but to share life, to pray, to remember, to hope. Faith did not begin with a statement of belief. It began with an encounter: the risen Christ in the midst of a broken, bewildered, joyful people.

This order matters. The pattern of Christian truth is not imposed from above but emerges from within the lived experience of the Church. Doctrine follows the shape of the Gospel itself, emerging from encounter with the risen Christ, nourished in communion, and finding expression in the confessions of the faithful. What the Church believes, teaches, and confesses is none other than the Gospel. It does not invent the truth; it responds to the truth already received.

Doctrine arises as the Church gives witness to what it has already received and experienced in the Spirit. This means doctrine does not make the Church; it would violate the pattern of Christian truth to suggest otherwise. Rather, the Church believes because it trusts that it belongs to Christ. The Church does not believe in order to belong. It is already grafted into the living, breathing Body of Christ, aflame with the Spirit.

From this communion of belonging, the Church gives voice to what it knows in the marrow of its being: that Jesus

Christ is Lord, that God is love, and that the Spirit is still moving. Creeds and doctrines do not manufacture belief, they confess it. The Creed does not make or define the Church; the Spirit gives birth to both. The Church, alive in the Spirit, gives voice to the truth of the Gospel as she confesses her faith through the Creed and not because of it.

The Church as the "new habitation of God in the Spirit," says John Wesley, was always meant to reflect the unity and communion of the Triune life. Its first creeds bore witness not only to what Christians believed, but to how they belonged. Doctrine was not just a description of faith. It was the grammar of love, a way of speaking and living that shapes the Church's identity, relationships, and practices for participation in God through faith.

A living tradition becomes an idol when it becomes the focus of its worship, a token when it becomes disconnected from the tradition and misguided in its worship, but an icon when it participates in the reality to which it points in its worship. When doctrine is grounded in communion and prayer, it serves as an icon, participating in divine love; but when separated from the Spirit's life in the Church, it can degenerate into a token or even an idol. In this sense, the creeds are not meant to be closed off by walls but opened windows that open us to mystery. They offer a shared language, forged in prayer and communion, language that arises not as boundary but as invitation, echoing this chapter's claim that doctrine emerges from the Church's lived experience of the Spirit. Through this experience, the Church sings, laments and proclaims the love of God that holds all things together.

This is why John Wesley could speak of the ontological priority of God's love in all things. For Wesley, doctrine was never meant to silence or exclude, but to speak with the language of faith, enliven hope, and express holy love. The Spirit that ignited the Church at Pentecost continues to kindle in us the same fire of God's love: a faith that begins in communion and flows outward into confession, into doxology, into life together in love. Doctrine, then, is the faithful grammar of divine love, a grammar that prepares the

Church to receive and respond to the Spirit who gives the words we speak in faith, a Spirit-given response that arises from the Church's communion with God, not as a prerequisite to faith but as its unfolding expression.

The Spirit Gives the Words

The Spirit who gives the Church her life also gives her faithful language. Doctrine does not begin within the academy or at the council table. It begins when someone, somewhere, opens their heart to God and finds the Spirit already praying within them. As Paul writes, "The Spirit intercedes with sighs too deep for words" (Romans 8:26).

Doctrine always begins in prayer because the first beginning of faith in the heart is trust, a trust that, while deeply personal, is always shaped and expanding by the communal life of the Church, her worship, and the Spirit-breathed memory of God's people. Trust is the purest form of faith, and this gift of faith is the bedrock foundation of love. It is the trust that we are known and loved by God.

Even when we ask for faith because we do not yet know it, the asking itself is a sign that the Spirit is already at work in us. Before we know what to believe, we know what it is to long, to groan, and to reach for God. That longing is already a kind of knowing, a knowing born from the Spirit's deepest work of faith in us. This is how doctrine begins in prayer, a trust that, while deeply personal, is always shaped and expanding by the communal life of the Church, her worship, and the Spirit-breathed memory of God's people.

John Wesley understood this well. He consistently asked, "Is your faith filled with the energy of God's love?" For Wesley, true faith is always a gift of the Spirit, and its evidence is not reduced to a set of right beliefs but through the holy love of God that permeates all creation. Both John and his brother Charles called this "catholic love," love that flows from the Triune life of God and embraces all. Catholic love is the soul of the Church's doctrine, functioning as the theological grounding for a doctrine that is expansive rather than restrictive, a love that calls the Church to embrace diversity, embody hospitality, and confess faith in a way that echoes the inclusive heart of the Triune God, a love that is expansive, inclusive, and missional, flowing from the life of the Triune God and reaching outward to embrace the whole of creation in grace and fellowship.

This was expressed through the poetry of Charles Wesley and the hymnody of the early Methodists, which gave voice to the deep affections of hearts awakened by grace. His poetry gave voice to what hearts awakened by the Spirit already knew: that the Trinity is not a puzzle to be solved, but a doxology to be sung. Charles knew that we do not reason our way to God. We are drawn by beauty, awakened by joy, and summoned by love.

Faith, once awakened by the Spirit, cannot remain silent. It burns to speak from the flame of love. And what it speaks are not mere propositions but praise. Faithful doctrine, in this light, is not the product of deduction or calculation. It is the fruit of communion. It is the Church, breathing deeply with the Spirit, giving language to the love it has received, a Spirit-formed grammar of communion that shapes how the Church knows, prays, and lives in faithful response.

This is why doctrine cannot be separated from the affective life of the Spirit, it is born where trust meets love, where longing becomes language. Doctrine does not answer longing with closure, but with communion, one that anticipates the Spirit's outpouring at Pentecost, where the language of love found many tongues. It teaches us how to listen to our deepest groanings and to respond in the grammar of grace. To teach doctrine, then, is not to explain the mystery of God but to invite others into the song. It is to say, "Come, let us sing to the Lord; let us make a joyful noise to the rock of our salvation" (Psalm 95:1). It is to say, "Taste and see" (Psalm 34:8). Come and listen. Come and sing.

This is why the Pentecost story is so central. The outpouring of the Spirit was not a silent event. How could a mighty rushing wind and the noise of many different tongues be quiet? Pentecost, that "new habitation of God in the Spirit," (Wesley) brings into the world many different ways of capturing the mystery of the infinite vulnerable love that is God. And in each tongue, the Gospel found a new accent, a new cadence, a new way to say, "God is love." This multiplicity is not a threat to unity but its fulfillment, reflecting the relational unity of the Trinity, diverse yet one in love. Doctrine shaped by the Spirit mirrors this harmony, inviting the Church to speak in many tongues with one heart. The Spirit does not erase difference but transfigures it into harmony. The Church does not confess in one tongue so much as she celebrates the gift of diversity and sings in harmony, many voices, one love.

To teach doctrine, then, is not to explain the mystery of God, but to invite others into the song, a song whose melody is shaped by the Spirit, and whose harmony resounds with the life of the Triune God. And the source of this song, the melody and harmony of our confession, is the Triune God whose love dwells in us. The Spirit who gives us the diverse languages of unitive love is the same Spirit who draws us into the very life of Father, Son, and Holy Spirit, "Trinity" in Unity and Unity in Trinity (Athanasius).

Doctrine as a Gift of the Triune Life

Doctrine does not originate in abstraction; it emerges from the heart of Trinitarian love, an affective rhythm of divine communion that echoes the Spirit's song already stirring within the Church. Both Charles and John Wesley taught that "until the whole Trinity descends into our faithful hearts," we cannot fully awaken to the transforming power of grace. The faithful heart that trusts is a participation in God's own trusting life and love, a Trinitarian movement in which the Spirit draws believers into the intimate trust shared between the Son and the Father, forming us within the very rhythms of divine communion and grounding our faith in the lived experience of grace that John Wesley so vividly described as the indwelling love of God.

In Charles Wesley's hymn "O Love Divine, How Sweet Thou Art," we hear this longing for the fullness of Triune indwelling: "Fixt on the Athanasian mound, I still require a firmer ground / That only can suffice for me, / The whole mysterious Trinity / Inhabiting my heart." Faith is not simply knowledge about God. It is God dwelling in us, and we in God. This is where we begin to speak the faithful grammar of God's love.

This is the logic of the Incarnation, the embodied pattern of divine revelation and participation. Jesus did not come to teach an abstract and detached doctrine. Jesus came to live the love of God in human flesh. In doing so, Christ revealed not only who God is, but what it means to be truly human. The descent of the Spirit at Pentecost continues this incarnational logic. The Spirit inhabits the Body of Christ, not as a vague presence, but as the fire of love poured into human hearts.

Furthermore, the soteriologic of the Gospel reveals the pattern by which faith, hope, and love are received and lived. Just as we are called to be holy as God is holy, or to be perfect as our heavenly Father is perfect, we know that all that God commands, God also gives and fulfills. Thus, doctrine that is the faithful grammar of God's love is formed from the logic of divine grace. We only love because God first loved us; we are only holy because God makes us holy. As such, Christ's own faithfulness (*pistis Christou*) becomes the source and shape of our faithful knowing and loving, grounding the development of doctrine not in human initiative but in Christ's perfect trust and love. This participatory model reveals doctrine as a Spirit-formed response, an echo of Christ's own relational fidelity lived out in the Church. As Paul says, "I live by the faithfulness of the Son of God, who loved me and gave himself for me" (Galatians 2:20).

When doctrine is untethered from this logic of divine initiative, it becomes "bad code," a disordered script lacking the Spirit's syntax of love that alone can animate faith in practice, like a corrupted algorithm that misguides our living. But when grounded in the Gospel, faithful doctrine becomes living code: a Spirit-infused pattern for knowing, loving, and acting. It is catechesis written in the grammar of God's love.

This is why John Wesley often spoke of the new birth as the Triune God making a home in the heart. Salvation is not only forgiveness; it is the divine indwelling, which makes us new creatures. And that indwelling always overflows. It gives birth to holy affections, to works of mercy, to the habits of prayer, and to the doctrines that name the perfect love of God that we trust. The work of faith is to trust in the indwelling love that not only forgives but invites us to partake of the love of God that inflames our hearts and makes us new creatures.

Doctrine, then, is not something the Church creates. It is something the Spirit draws forth. It is the way love takes shape in language of faithful hearts.

It is the Church's attempt to name what it means to be caught up in the Triune life of God, an act always provisional, always unfolding, as the Church is continually drawn deeper into the mystery of divine love by the Spirit. We believe who we trust because we know to whom we belong, and when we know that we belong we will confess what we believe and trust about the One to whom we belong. Doctrine is the grammar of that belonging when the Spirit pours the energy of God's love into our hearts.

Gregory of Nazianzus, often called "The Theologian," for his profound theological insights, gave particular attention to how we must be careful how we speak about God who in essence is beyond human comprehension. In his *Theological Orations*, Gregory warns that we must "be still," as in prayer, to know God because our human ways of knowing God are "faint and feeble." And yet, to be silent is to neglect the truth that emerges from the stillness. This conviction echoes through the Church's history and reminds us that doctrine is not simply intellectual; it is doxological. It arises from divine indwelling and is meant to glorify the God who dwells among us.

The Holy Spirit does not simply clarify doctrine; the Spirit makes it possible. The Spirit is the condition for the possibility of all faithful speech about God. Without the Spirit, we lack the words to speak of faith, and then our doctrine becomes brittle, reduced to argument or ideology, cut off from the Spirit's dynamic and doxological speech that enlivens the Church's witness and calls the church into deeper communion. But when forged in the fire of God's love, it becomes a living word, a gift that binds us to Christ and to each other.

- 17 -

In this way, doctrine is not external to salvation; it is one of its fruits. Doctrine is not the way into grace, but the expression of a life full of faith embraced by grace. And that grace is nothing less than the life of the Triune God shared with the world, through Christ, in the Spirit.

From Dogma to Living Faith

In this chapter, I use terms like doctrine, dogma, creed, and grammar of love to describe the Church's faithful attempt to speak of the divine love she has received. Though distinct in theological nuance, these terms all serve a common purpose: to help the Church give voice to the faith that lives in communion with the Triune God.

The word "dogma" has come to sound cold in many ears, evoking rigidity, exclusion, or control rather than awe, love and witness. Yet originally, dogma functioned as the Church's doxological confession, a Spirit-born proclamation shaped in prayer and communion, not as a fixed point, or an inflexible demand. Dogma in its earliest sense, was never about rigidity. It was about the Church's faithful witness to the mystery of God revealed in Christ. Dogma was never meant to constrain; it was meant to confess the faith of Christ the Church had received, a faith born in the Spirit and encountered in communion, not constructed as episcopal control.

The Church's dogma is her faith. The Creeds are not marginal additions to the Christian life; they are the distilled memory of the Church, preserved and enlivened by the Spirit, who carries the Church's lived experience of God through struggle, grace, and prayer, a memory formed in prayer, clarified through struggle, and sustained by love. They were never meant to end conversation but to deepen communion. When dogma lives, it serves the Church as a means of grace, offering language that both grounds and guides the community in its journey toward God.

The essence of faith is love, and the grammar of that love is faithful doctrine. Doctrine and faith go hand-in-hand, for what the Church believes is not static proposition but dynamic communion, animated by the Spirit and expressed through the grammar of love that shapes the Church's shared life in Christ. The Creeds give voice to that faith, and the Church confesses them not to belong, but because she already belongs. The Spirit, who has gifted the Church with the Faith of Christ, continues to draw her into deeper participation in the love of God. And because this love is infinite and vulnerable, it is always growing and changing, and expanding in time, in place, and in flesh.

In the New Testament, the Pauline phrase "faith of Christ" (*pistis Christou*) is a deeply participatory understanding of salvation. It is not just faith in Christ, but the faithfulness of Christ, the lived trust and obedience of the Son to the Father, into which the Church is drawn. This distinction is central to understanding doctrine as not merely belief about God but a participation in the very faith that Christ exercises in trust and love. As Christ trusts in the Spirit so must the Church. Otherwise, when the Church stops breathing in the Spirit who makes the Church to be Christ's living breathing Body, she loses faith and the capacity to speak in the grammar of love and eventually dies.

John Wesley knew that faith is not ours to possess, but God's to give. He did not reduce faith to mental assent. Rather, he saw true faith as a living trust in the love of God poured into our hearts by the Spirit. This is why he insisted that all doctrine must be "practical divinity," language shaped by grace and aimed toward holy love. Faithful doctrine must take on flesh and live in the world for its life.

Yet dogma can become distorted. When it becomes a tool for exclusion or domination, it ceases to function as a means of grace. It hardens. It forgets the Spirit. It becomes traditionalism, what Jaroslav Pelikan called "the dead faith of the living." Yet tradition is also developmental, like a body growing into maturity under the guidance of the Spirit, who draws the Church into ever-deepening participation in the unfolding love and eschatological promise of God. Doctrine does not abandon its origins and convictions but deepens them as it grows, recapitulating the truth of God in Christ through the Spirit (God's "two hands," Christ and the Spirit) in ever-expanding fullness. This vision of growth affirms that doctrine is not static but is an unfolding participation in the Spirit's work, maturing with the Church as it is drawn more deeply into the love and mystery of the Triune God. This hopeful vision invites the Church to embody faith and trust that the Spirit will not let the doctrines of faith decay but faithfully lead the Church into a more complete participation in the mystery of Christ. "Wherever the Spirit is there is the Church of Christ," exclaims St. Irenaeus (*Against Heresies*).

The problem is not that the Church has dogma. The problem arises when that dogma no longer participates in the living tradition of the Church, when it forgets that the Holy Spirit is the animating force of tradition, breathing vitality and grace into its witness across generations, when it ceases to breathe with the Spirit's vitality. This rupture occurs when we forget that the living, breathing Body of Christ, the Church catholic, is called to grow and change as it is drawn into the promise of New Creation. And just as the Church matures and changes, so too must the canonical gifts of the Spirit, the Scriptures and the Creeds, participate in that unfolding transformation. They are not static artifacts but living witnesses to the infinite vulnerable love of God, shaped by and shaping the Spirit-born journey toward God's promised future.

The Church does not discard or replace the Creeds, any more than it discards or replaces the canon of Scripture. But it must be forever reforming in its faithful use of these canonical gifts. For they do not contain the fullness of God's infinite, vulnerable love; rather, they point toward it, propel us into it, and at times must themselves be reinterpreted in light of it. The promise of God entrusted to us in Scripture and Creed calls for Spirit-led correction, not to erase the past, but to fulfill it more faithfully. Across the Church's history, there are moments when inherited uses must give way to new renderings, when the Spirit compels the Body to repent, to re-see, and to re-speak what has been handed down. From the re-reading of Torah in the letter to the Hebrews, to the lived realities of today's Church, this pattern holds. "Future glory has already begun," John Wesley reminds us. Nothing of the Church's faith, past, present, or future, is lost or discarded.

But all is transfigured and renewed, that it may flourish in the light of New Creation.

Faith does not grow evenly or uniformly or universally the same for everyone on a single timetable. Love takes root in varied ways, in diverse voices, at different times. But it always grows, and it always changes as it stretches, according to the expansive energy of divine, cruciform love. The Triune Creator has entrusted to the Church the faithful use of these gifts, these means of grace, as instruments through which we are drawn toward our final glory in communion with God. The future of creation and the Church and the future of God hinges on this sacred trust. And in the words of Charles Wesley, we rest assured: "The Spirit will not let us miss providence's way." The Spirit will be faithful. Therefore, the Church must also be faithful, "doing no harm" (Wesley) to the growing convictions and vibrant diversity of tongues that seek to speak with a faith energized by the love of God.

The truth handed down in the Church matures with those who receive it. Doctrine, like creation, recapitulates, reaching its fullness through time as the Church is drawn more fully into the mystery it confesses. The infinite love of God cannot be exhausted or contained by any one generation's doctrine. This is why the Spirit's work is not to discard what has been handed down, but to illumine it, expand it, and write it anew into the hearts and imaginations of the faithful. The means of grace, Scripture, Creeds, sacraments, icons, saints, are not barriers to growth, but launchpads into the mystery of God's love.

This is why doctrine must be spoken from the fire of love, or not at all. For only when doctrine is kindled in the shared life of communion, rather than imposed as control, does it bear faithful witness to the God who is love. Only when the words are forged in prayer, in worship, and in the shared life of the Church, do they bear faithful witness to the One who is love. Doctrine is not a fortress to defend but a flame to tend, and to share.

Doctrine in the Rhythm of Grace

Faithful doctrine must never become untethered from the Church; it must always grow within it. Doctrine is not imposed from above or fabricated in isolation, it arises, as earlier affirmed, from the Church's shared life of belonging, shaped by communion and sustained by love. It is discerned in the rhythm of worship, prayer, and shared life. It is forged in community, refined by love, and animated by the Spirit.

John Wesley understood this deeply. For him, faith was never an individual achievement, but a gift of grace that comes wrapped in the Good News and grows and evolves as a communal song. This is why he insisted on class meetings, band meetings, and societies, because faithful doctrine grows best in circles of vulnerable trust and abiding friendship, where Scripture is wrestled with, prayer is shared, and love is practiced. Doctrine arises not outside of grace and humility, but as a grace taking form through the language of faithful knowing through love, a grammar of love discerned in community and shaped by the Spirit's ongoing work of illuminating God's truth through worship, prayer, and shared life. The rich wisdom of the Church's doctrines illuminates the many ways of knowing through love.

In the Wesleyan vision, the means of grace are not merely disciplines, they are God's own generous self-giving to form Christ in us. We do not reason our way to truth; we are drawn into it by the Spirit, together. Wesley's notion that God's commands are clothed in God's promises follows Augustine's prayer and powerfully echoes the chapter's larger theme that God gives what God commands through the Spirit's enabling grace in his *Confessions*: "Grant what you command, and command what you will." As such, the doctrines of the Church are means of grace that embody the faith of Christ that is filled with the energy of God's love to ensure that we speak the grammar of love and reach God's promised end in New Creation. Doctrine, in this light, is not cold regulation through rigid codes of conduct or absolute categories of thought but Spirit-infused articulation, a grammar of belonging that invites us into relationship with the Triune God. It is shaped by God's grace and ordered toward the perfect love of God.

Doctrine must not be understood as abstract formulas but as embodied formation, seen, for example, in baptismal catechesis, eucharistic liturgy, or communal lament, woven into the Church's practices of prayer, mercy, worship, and communal discernment that shape lives in grace. The Church is a habitat of grace, and doctrine is one of her living practices. Just as we learn to pray, to show mercy, and to worship, so too we learn to confess our love and gratitude to God and all creation. Doctrine is not first an act of intellectual apprehension or "a priori" logic, but a language received in love. Just as we love because we are first loved by God, so we know because we are first known by God. The grammar of faith born from love becomes the Church's language of faith that is always shaped by grace.

And because doctrine grows and develops within the Body of Christ, its aim is never finished perfection, but perfect love that perseveres, in hope and in faithful trust in the promises of God. Doctrine is not a weapon to wield or a code of thinking to defend; it is a means of grace pointing us toward God's promised end. It teaches us how to walk in the way of love, and how to walk together. It nurtures the Church's journey in hope and trust, guiding hearts toward communion rather than conformity, inviting a shared life of grace and discernment over rigid enforcement, and fostering mutual transformation rather than uniform agreement. It teaches us how to trust with the same faith and trust of Christ. Doctrine without trust is nothing more than bad code, a distortion that betrays the very faith Christ gave to the Church.

The Church is Christ's living, breathing Body, animated by the Spirit and rooted in the communion of the Triune God. The doctrines of the Church must breathe with the same Spirit that breathes the Church into being. They must remain flexible, humble, and always open to the Spirit's refining fire. If our doctrines do not lead us to greater mercy, deeper humility, and more joy, for the life of the world, then we have ceased to listen to the One who speaks through them.

Doctrine belongs to the Church not as an artifact, but as a living companion on the Spirit-led pilgrimage toward God's future, animated by the Spirit, who guides and renews the Church's understanding as she journeys ever deeper into the mystery of divine love. As we walk that road together, we carry doctrine not as a relic of certainty, but as a witness to grace: not control, but love; not fear, but joy; not pride, but trust.

The Future of Doctrine

Doctrine is not the end of the conversation, it is the invitation to begin anew, echoing the Spirit's yearning for a new grammar of love that rises from hope and communion, an openness that flows from the Spirit's ongoing work of drawing the Church into deeper faithfulness and love, a first word in the unfolding dialogue of divine love that stretches across time and space. The language of faith must always be held with humility and wonder, because the One we confess is inexhaustible. Doctrine that forgets its provisional character becomes brittle, more concerned with preservation than transformation.

The Spirit is not done speaking. Doctrine must remain open to the ongoing work of the Spirit, just as the Church discerned in the Council of Jerusalem (Acts 15) how Gentiles might be welcomed into the community of faith without adherence to the full Mosaic Law. That moment of discernment, where the apostles confessed, "it seemed good to the Holy Spirit and to us," remains a model of doctrinal openness: listening to the Spirit, the tradition, and the lived witness of the community in the life of the Church and the world. This is not to say that everything is always up for grabs, but that the Church must always be listening, discerning the voice of the Spirit through the cries of the world, the beauty of creation, the witness of the saints, and the breath of prayer. The Church is God's new way of being in the world, the dwelling of the Spirit, called to speak not only from what has been but toward what shall be.

The inseparability of past, present, and future is fundamental to how doctrine lives, reflecting the character of

God's love, unfolding yet consistent, ever faithful and ever new. The Word who spoke all things into existence is the same Word who became flesh and promises to make all things new. The Creator did not simply form creation as a static container for divine action, but as the very place in which God would share and entrust God's future with the whole of creation.

From the beginning to the end, creation is always suffused with God's love, love that binds past and future without separation, forming to grow, evolve, and expand in the same manner that God has chosen to grow, evolve, and expand in communion with creation. From the first breath of the Creator to the future Word of New Creation, everything lives, moves, and breathes with the energy of divine love. This is why our end is already present in our beginning, and our beginning awaits its promised fulfillment in the end. Doctrine lives in this same eschatological tension. It is never final or fixed, because God's love is ever-unfolding. Doctrine must grow and change, not to betray its past, but to fulfill the depth of its calling through the guiding presence of the Holy Spirit, who leads the Church ever deeper into the mystery of divine love: a calling rooted in love as the Church's interpretive lens, and in tradition as participatory communion with the Spirit who draws the Church deeper into the mystery of Christ across time: to bear witness to love that is always becoming more.

When we truly hear the Word, we are compelled to respond, not with repetition, but with a new word. Doctrine, then, is not an echo of the spoken Word, but a faithful conversation that is a participation in the divine love that is always speaking and summoning and desiring our faithful response of love. It is the Church speaking back to God and to the world with the language of faith that is continually stretched by love, transfigured by prayer, and open to the inbreaking of the Spirit.

John Wesley taught that all of God's future promises are present in every command, underscoring his vision of grace as divine initiative that enables human response and tying together the Church's eschatological hope with its Spirit-empowered participation in the unfolding of divine love. In other words, when God speaks it happens, and the promised future of God is already happening. Hope, therefore, is not a vague sentiment of wishful thinking; it is the Spirit's active presence drawing us toward the promised fullness of perfect love. Doctrine, when it lives in this faith-filled hope, becomes a vessel of imagination and courageous love. Truth is never separable from beauty and goodness, doctrine must be radiant with the splendor of divine love if it is to bear faithful witness. His vision of theological aesthetics reminds us that doctrine cannot merely inform; it must inspire, illuminate, and invite us into the drama of God's love unfolding in history and hope. Doctrine, when shaped by love and transfigured by beauty, becomes a harmony that reveals the radiance of God's truth, a symphony of faithful speech that participates in doxology, joining the Church's worship and praise of the Triune God (Truth is , as Hans Urs von Balthasar has often sid, symphonic!). To speak doctrine, then, is to reflect the beauty of God's loving self-gift to the world.

In this light, doctrine is not about final answers or finished creeds. It is about faithful speech that is forged in love. It is about witnessing to the infinite vulnerable love that is God from everlasting to everlasting. Continuity and change mark the vibrancy and health of the Church's faith that aspires to speak with the grammar of God's love. Doctrine always changes, grows, and evolves when it is formed by love. How could it not? Doctrine that grows in love helps correct the tradition and safeguard it from becoming dead faith as it moves forward into the promise of New Creation. But faithful doctrine also grows in continuity with the living faith of the tradition. Such doctrinal change amidst the ebb and flow of life does not simply abandon traditional doctrinal formulations for the sake of change; rather, it carries the faith of the past forward, allowing the living tradition to deepen and widen as the Spirit draws the Church more fully into the mystery of God's future. Eschatological hope is what keeps the doctrines of faith alive, and the energy of God's love animates them toward their doxological end.

Theological hope looks forward to a time when doctrine and love are one song, when all tongues will confess and every voice will rise in harmony. This is the promise of New Creation. Doctrine, at its best, participates in this promise not by closing the book, but by turning the page.

This is why doctrine must be spoken from the fire of love, or not spoken at all, for only then can it become doctrine made flesh, a faithful witness to the love that burns at the heart of God's future. Just as all creation groans with longing to behold the face of God and to receive the words of infinite, vulnerable love from the inbreaking of New Creation, so too does God yearn, joyfully, expectantly, to hear from us a brand-new grammar of love. Doctrine, if it is to be faithful, must rise from this shared yearning: the Spirit-breathed utterance of a people transfigured by hope, learning to speak again in the language of glory.

Faithful doctrine is only spoken from the fire of love. For the whole creation groans to see the face of the Father, to hear the voice of the Son, to breathe with the Spirit who brings the world to life. From the depths of our longing and the heights of God's mercy, love speaks, risking new words, stretching old forms, kindling a grammar no longer bound by fear but freed by grace. And just as God speaks, Father, Son, and Holy Spirit, so too does God yearn to hear from us: a new sound rising from the communion of saints, a language born of wounded joy and radiant hope, a doctrine transfigured by the love that makes all things new.

Chapter Two
Doctrine as the Language of Spirit-Born Faith

The Need to Speak, Faith Reaches for Language

Faith, once awakened by the Spirit, cannot remain silent. It burns to speak from the flame of God's love. As Augustine affirms in the *Confessions* (X.6.8), the soul that loves God longs to sing. This longing to sing is rooted in his deeper theology of desire and memory, where memory is not merely recollection, but the soul's interior chamber where God dwells and speaks. Doctrine, in this light, is the Church's faithful act of remembering in love, naming and responding to what the Spirit has awakened in the soul. Just as Augustine's heart was restless until it found rest in God, so too does doctrine arise from the heart's desire to name and praise the God who first loved us. Just as the Word speaks all creation into existence, this same Word is the Love that is God, and this Love that embodies faith seeks expression. As faith begins to speak with the grammar of grace, it does not begin as an intellectual assent to belief or even an apprehension of abstract ideas. Faith begins by reaching outward to speak in acts of mercy and compassion and, when necessary, with words of meaning and gratitude for such indescribable love.

Faith is always seeking a language, not to control mystery, but to respond to the infinite, vulnerable love of God that grows within the hearts of believers. It is the desire to name what has been felt, to confess what has been revealed, to praise the God who has already spoken. Doctrine begins here: faith reaching for words in the wake of God's love. And Scripture, the Spirit-breathed testimony to God's action in the world, offers the Church its foundational language of love.

Creed as Confession, Early Language of Love

The Church's earliest creeds were not instruments of control. They were confessions of wonder, language formed in the heart of a praying people, shaped in the furnace of worship, witness, persecution, and praise. Before doctrine was defined, faith was confessed.

"The Rule of Faith" (*regula fidei*), a phrase used by Irenaeus and Tertullian, was not a checklist, but a living memory of the Church's encounter with the God revealed in Jesus Christ. It was passed down in doxological form, repeated in baptismal liturgies, whispered by martyrs, and sung in catacombs. As Irenaeus articulates in *Against Heresies* (1:10.1; 3:4.2), this transmission was not a sterile rehearsal of dogma but the living memory of love, doctrine shaped by the Church's intimate encounter with the crucified and risen Christ. For Irenaeus, the rule of faith was a safeguard against distortion not through coercion, but by anchoring the Church's proclamation in the narrative of divine love revealed in Jesus. It was theology as memory, not manipulation; doctrine as love remembering.

Creeds began as communal prayers that held the heart of the Gospel in the midst of competing claims and creeping distortions. The Apostles' Creed and the Nicene Creed emerged not from a thirst for control but from a pastoral need to voice shared faith in the Triune God. Each creed arose from distinct historical and ecclesial circumstances, responding to theological confusion, pastoral concern, and the need to preserve unity in the face of growing diversity within the early Church. These creeds were the Church's poetry of belief, carefully crafted responses to divine love.

Even before the formal creeds, there was another creed pulsing in the earliest gatherings, a confession St. Paul may be quoting in Galatians 3:28: "There is no longer Jew or Greek... for all of you are one in Christ Jesus." Galatians 3:28 challenged the prevailing social hierarchies by dissolving ethnic, social, and gender distinctions in Christ. It redefined belonging not by Roman citizenship or patriarchal order, but by baptism into a radically inclusive community shaped by the Spirit's liberating love. This early Pauline confession proclaimed a new identity grounded in divine solidarity and ecclesial equality. It proclaimed belonging, reshaped identity, and grounded unity in God's love.

Doctrine was never meant to divide, but to unify. It expressed the reality of a people who had become a new creation, a living Body of Christ, rooted in the unity of the Triune God. John Wesley echoed this in calling the Church "the new habitation of God in the Spirit," a phrase grounded in his *Notes* on Ephesians 2:22, where he interprets this as the Spirit forming believers into a dwelling place for God through mutual indwelling and love, where he emphasizes the Spirit's indwelling presence among the faithful. This idea is also reflected in his sermons, such as "The Catholic Spirit" and "Scriptural Christianity," where Wesley links true faith not to institutional forms but to a community animated by divine love and holy conversation. For Wesley, doctrine was never detached from this communal and Spirit-filled vision of the Church. Doctrine, then, is love's language of communion, with God, each other, and all creation.

Creeds, at their best, say: We have seen the Lord. We have known His love. This is our witness. They bow before mystery. They are the Church's words for the unspeakable, formed in worship and prayer.

John Wesley valued the historic creeds, but not as gates of orthodoxy to be policed. His inclusion of the Apostles' Creed in the 1784 Sunday Service of the Methodists demonstrates how he understood creeds as instruments of devotion and formation rather than exclusion. He saw them as guides to devotion. He included the Apostles' Creed in Methodist worship not as a test, but as a means of grace. Creeds, for Wesley, belonged in the language of prayer and holy living.

The same is true of Charles Wesley's hymns, which function as lyrical creeds. For example, in "And Can It Be," Wesley proclaims, "My chains fell off, my heart was free, I rose, went forth, and followed thee," a creedal statement of liberation, justification, and discipleship in poetic form. "And can it be," "Love divine," and "Come, Thou long-expected Jesus" are sung confessions, powerful not for doctrinal precision alone, but for their doxological longing.

To speak of the Church's creeds as doxological confession leads naturally to a deeper question: how does the

Church sustain, form, and transmit this language of love across generations? The answer is doctrine, faith's grammar of belonging, forged in communion and lived in community.

Doctrine as the Grammar of Belonging

When considering the creeds as the Church's early confessions of love, the question naturally emerges: how is such a language learned and sustained? Doctrine functions as the grammar of this faith, holding together identity, memory, and community in Spirit-formed speech. Drawing on theological voices who deepen this vision can help us see doctrine not only as grammar, but as formation, imagination, and communion.

If the Church's faith confessed in the Creed is a poetry of love, then certainly the doctrines of the Church's faith contain the grammar of belonging. It is not about creating doctrinal boundaries for their own sake, it is about making space for communion, conversation, and imagination. Doctrine gives the Church a way to name its life in God, to preserve its memory, and to pass on its faith in language that invites rather than excludes.

This grammar is not detached from life; it is learned through belonging. Doctrine is not simply propositional. It is relational. It does not function merely to state what is true, but to form a people who live truthfully in love. This is why doctrine is learned in community; it is caught as much as it is taught. Doctrinal confession is never just cognitive but profoundly trustful, it is an act of trusting the God who makes himself known in relationship, forming the Church's moral and relational imagination, it shapes how we live with one another before it defines what we believe. It is relational, participatory, and rooted in the community's worship and witness. The goal is not mastery but participation. To know the doctrines of the Church is not merely to recite them, but to be drawn into their music, their movement, their meaning.

This is why doctrinal vitality depends on the Spirit's presence. When the ecclesial space for evolving conversations in faith and imagination is lost, doctrine becomes static and restricting, and soon, it begins to choke out the life of faith filled with the animus of love. Doctrine that no longer breathes is no longer faithful. It must remain supple, responsive, and rooted in the ongoing communion of the Spirit.

Theologian George Lindbeck called doctrine a "cultural-linguistic framework," contrasting it with the more propositional approaches of evangelical theology and the experiential focus of liberal theology. His model emphasizes that doctrine is less about stating objective truths or expressing inner experience, and more about inhabiting a community's language and practices that form a coherent way of life, a kind of grammar by which the Church learns to speak truthfully about God and faithfully about itself. In *The Nature of Doctrine*, Lindbeck contrasts three models of doctrine: the cognitive-propositional model, which sees doctrine as a set of universal truth statements; the experiential-expressive model, which views doctrine as the symbolic articulation of inner religious experience; and the cultural-linguistic model, which treats doctrine as the communal language and grammar that forms a religious way of life. This latter model highlights how doctrine functions not primarily to express propositions or feelings, but to shape communal identity and theological imagination within a living tradition. Like any language, doctrine is learned in community, through liturgy, Scripture, sacrament, and service. The goal is not simply to know the right words, but to be formed by them, to let love speak through the shared language of faith.

Such love preserves memory without becoming rigid. In this sense, doctrine not only speaks but also trains the Church to live into its deepest loves. Jaroslav Pelikan reminded us that "tradition is the living faith of the dead," while "traditionalism is the dead faith of the living." Doctrine lives when it breathes, when it is allowed to speak in new tongues and to resonate with the experiences of every generation. Doctrine, in its truest sense, is tradition alive, faith still speaking, still responding to the Spirit's presence in the Church.

Doctrine is never only about ideas. It is about identity, memory, and relationship. It tells us who we are, whose we are, and how we are to live. The early Church did not develop doctrine in abstraction, it did so to remain faithful to the God they had come to know in Christ and to preserve the unity of love that the Spirit had created among them.

Doctrine, then, is the grammar of love, spoken not only about God, but in God. Doctrinal formations emerge from contemplative depths, not only shaping language, but also illuminating the theological significance of gender, power, and ecclesial identity, from prayerful openness to the Spirit, where desire, silence, and communion shape faithful language. Contemplation is not passive withdrawal but a transformative posture that generates theological clarity and doctrinal insight. From this perspective, prayer becomes the crucible in which language about God is purified, shaped, and sustained. It draws us into the rhythm of the Trinity, a divine communion of mutual giving and receiving. And as John Wesley insisted, right doctrine is not about speculation, but about transformation. It is meant to renew our minds, shape our hearts, and empower us to live holy lives marked by love.

This is why, for Wesley, the test of doctrine was always its fruit in the life of the believer and the community. If it did not build up, edify, and sanctify, it was to be reexamined. Love was the measure.

At the same time, Wesley understood the risks. Doctrine becomes dangerous when it is lifted out of community, unmoored from love, and wielded as a tool of exclusion. But when doctrine stays rooted in prayer, praise, and sacramental life, it becomes language that draws us deeper into union with God and one another.

To confess doctrine, then, is not simply to state what we believe, it is to join in the shared speech of the Church. It is to say: this is who we are. This is how we live in love and establish our belonging.

Dogma and the Risk of Control

Dogma is the Church's confessed faith, the settled expression of the Church's deepest convictions about God's love and the shape of salvation. But when dogma is mistaken as a tool for control rather than a witness of love, it becomes brittle and dangerous.

The rule of faith preceded and shaped the Church's formation of the canon of Scripture, emphasizing that it was the early Church's lived experience of the risen Christ that generated the canon's authority, not the reverse. This prior identity in Christ's faith and faithfulness is essential for any faithful reading and interpretation of Scripture. The Spirit is the source of the Church's rule of faith, which precedes both the Creeds and the Holy Scriptures. When the Church forgets this and begins to wield these gifts as instruments of institutional preservation rather than divine communion, it ceases to be a faithful steward of grace.

History offers sobering reminders: from the Inquisition to the theological rationalizations for colonial conquest and the enslavement of Indigenous peoples in doctrines like the "Doctrine of Discovery." Dogma has been misused to preserve power rather than serve love. And when that happens, sacraments suffer. When doctrinal boundaries become tools of exclusion, the font becomes a gate instead of a welcome, the table, a barrier instead of a feast. The exclusion of women and the laity from theological voice and leadership reveals how misuse of dogma undermines the Spirit's gifts to the whole Body.

Yet even here, grace calls us forward. The substance of faith is love, God's love. Not abstract truth claims, or conceptual ideas about God, but infinite and vulnerable love that is God. This means that the faith that is given to us by the energy of love is always unfolding and stretching; Truth is the infinite vulnerable love that is God. As we grow in communion with God, our expressions of faith must also grow and stretch. How could they not when our faith is filled with the energy of God's infinite vulnerable love?

Richard Hooker's often-cited "three-legged stool" of Scripture, Reason, and Tradition describes a structured hierarchy by which the Church's doctrine is grounded and develops through time. For Hooker, Scripture holds primary authority; reason, illuminated by grace, serves to interpret it; and tradition, as the Church's communal memory, is shaped and corrected by both. This model upheld the integrity of the Church's theological witness across generations. Yet it is crucial to recall that before there was a canon of Scripture or a Creed of the Church, there was the experience of the risen Christ, an encounter with the infinite, cruciform love of God. It is this Spirit-breathed encounter that birthed both faith and the Church's grammar of love. John Wesley, inheriting Hooker's Anglican framework, affirmed this structure but added experience as a vital dimension, not to privilege individual or private subjectivity, but to underscore that doctrine arises from the Spirit's ongoing work in lived encounter. In Wesley's view, theology begins not with abstract principles but with the transforming presence of the Triune God, who is to be known, loved, and worshipped.

However, as the Enlightenment placed increasing emphasis on rationality within the Church of England, doctrines like the Trinity were often sidelined, regarded more as intellectual puzzles than as invitations into divine life. It was precisely against this rationalistic tendency that William J. Abraham offered his well-known critique of the Wesleyan Quadrilateral that was popularized by Albert C. Outler. And in response, proposed "canonical theism," a theological framework grounded not in abstract criteria but in the lived practices and authoritative structures of the historic Church.

Abraham warned that when Scripture, Tradition, Reason, and Experience are treated as independent sources or criteria of truth, they foster theological hubris and dilute the primacy of divine revelation. Instead, Abraham argued, these four are best understood as means of grace, channels through which the Spirit draws the Church into communion with the living God. They possess no autonomous authority; their significance arises only insofar as they are enlivened by the Spirit. In this light, doctrine, when shaped in humility and grounded in love, becomes not a system of control but a participatory invitation into God's future. The Church's true authority is not the quadrilateral itself, but the God who speaks through it, and whose final Word, as Scripture testifies, is Love (1 John 4:8).

When doctrine is frozen, it becomes an idol. But when it breathes with the Spirit, it becomes a wellspring: forming faith, deepening communion, guiding the Church in love. Even our most cherished formulations must be held with open hands, always subject to the Spirit's refining work of love. Conservatism can preserve value, but when it refuses risk, it reveals a lack of faith. Faith lives by letting go and listening anew.

Dogma does not die when it is examined in love; it dies when treated as untouchable because it presumes to be certain of its faith and forgets that only the Spirit sustains doctrine as living truth in communion. The Church must remember: the Creeds are not ends in themselves. They are echoes of the Word, sacramental signs that point beyond themselves, as Wesley affirmed in their devotional use and as the Church Fathers often practiced in their doxological formulation. The Word can never be contained or exhausted. The Spirit is still speaking.

But dogma need not become dead weight. When rightly held, it returns to its origin in awe. The goal of all doctrine, after all, is not to master truth but to adore the God who is Love. We are drawn now to doctrine's deepest purpose: praise.

Doctrine as Doxology

If doctrine is the Church's language of faith, it must return to its deepest source: praise. All true speech about God must ultimately become doxology.

Doctrine is never just definition. At its best, it is devotion made intelligible. It is theology rising into prayer, reflection giving way to adoration. Charles Wesley's hymns are confessions set to music, lyrical creeds meant to be remembered in the heart.

For John Wesley, doctrine was not only what the Church believed, but how the Church believed. If doctrine does not lead to worship, something is missing. Doctrine becomes doxology when it moves from something we defend to something we delight in, not because we possess truth, but because we have been possessed by the Truth who is Love.

When doctrine forgets its doxological roots, it becomes defensive and dry. True doctrinal clarity arises not from polemical certainty but from contemplative openness, a stance especially vital in an age of doctrinal polarization, where prayerful attentiveness can open pathways to communion rather than division, a depth of prayerful attention that incorporates apophasis and gendered vulnerability as central to the theological task, the kind of loving attention in prayer that shapes the soul before it shapes the sentence. But when it remembers its source, it becomes a means of grace, helping us name the God who is still speaking.

Doctrine is prayer. It is the Church's long, unbroken prayer of trust, woven into its daily liturgy, voiced in its creeds, and sustained by the Spirit through centuries of praise. Every time we say, "I believe," we are entering relationship. We join our voices with the Church of every age in adoring the God who first loved us.

The is why the Trinitarian shape of Wesleyan faith matters deeply, it anchors doctrine in humility and praise, reminding us that all theological language flows from the mutual love of Father, Son, and Spirit. All comes from the Father, is revealed in the Son, and is poured into our hearts by the Spirit. This is the eternal circle of love that animates doctrine.

The final test of doctrine is not whether it is systematic, but whether it helps us love. Does it bring joy? Humility? Wonder? Can it still sing?

Doctrine is not a wall, it is a window. Not a cage, but a candle. As John Wesley taught, doctrine is a means of grace, a way through which the light of God's love shines into our lives, inviting us not to containment but to communion. It reflects the Light of the world. When it leads us to praise, to weep, to kneel, it has fulfilled its purpose.

And yet the Church does not live by memory alone. Just as doxology lifts its eyes toward promise, so too must faithful doctrine lean forward into hope. What, then, is the future of doctrine? What kind of faithful speech will serve the world yet to come?

Faith and Doctrine in the Church's Future

The Spirit of God is always leading the Church forward, not away from its foundations, but deeper into them. Like creation groaning for redemption in Romans 8, or the New Jerusalem descending in Revelation 21, the Church moves toward God's promised future not by retreating from its roots, but by pressing deeper into them with hope-filled expectancy. Doctrine, when faithful, becomes the echo of this forward pull, a witness to the Spirit who renews all things. Faithful doctrine always participates in this forward movement of creation's groaning and the promise of New Creation.

Jurgen Moltmann, the reowned author of *A Theology of Hope*, reminds us that "Christianity is eschatology" and that doctrine that resists change fails not simply because it is false, but more fundametally because it forgets that Christian truth propelled by the sustaining breezes of hope.

As we look to the future, we must ask: What kind of doctrine will speak to a wounded world? A world marked by ecological collapse, racial division, economic inequality, and spiritual disillusionment cries out not for abstractions but for embodied truth. Theologies of exclusion, triumphalism, or cold rationalism cannot heal such wounds. What is needed is doctrine that bends low in love, speaks in lament and hope, and testifies to the crucified and risen Christ whose wounds are now radiant with glory. Can our theology still invite trust, kindle joy, and proclaim belonging?

By the Spirit's power, the answer is yes.

Yes, because the creeds were born of love, and that love is still speaking. Yes, because the fire that kindled our doctrines has not gone out. Yes, because the Spirit that formed the Church is still leading her.

The future of doctrine belongs to those who receive the past as gift and promise, not as a relic to preserve but as a living seed to cultivate. This resonance opens space for new forms of doctrine shaped by the Spirit's presence in unexpected places, ecological theology that listens to creation's groaning, interfaith dialogue that honors mutual longing for truth, digital liturgies that carry praise across new frontiers. The future of doctrine will be voiced in many tongues and carried by communities who dare to believe that love always has more to say. Tradition lives not as repetition, but as resonance.

Geoffrey Wainwright once said that "theology, in order to be sound, must sing," a reflection of his conviction that worship and eschatological vision are not optional extras, but central to the vitality and soundness of doctrine. Doctrine must join the Church's eternal song, a doxology anticipating the fullness of love still to come.

John Wesley taught that the Church must always go on to perfection, not only as a personal aspiration, but as a communal calling shaped by shared practices of grace and love, not in pride, but in love. He envisioned a people whose doctrine was holy, whose hearts were aflame, whose lives were liturgies of grace.

So, we return to the Spirit and the Word. The Church exists not as an institution that guards truth, but as communion in the Spirit, a foretaste of the eschatological life where doctrine resonates with the freedom of divine love. To a Church gathered in prayer, aflame with divine affection, still learning to speak what love has made known. We return to doctrine as a Spirit-born language of hope and holy desire.

And so the Church sings:

We believe in Love made flesh,
Who spoke in fire and still whispers in flame.
We believe in the Spirit, ever new,
Breathing old truths into future tongues and future truths into old ones.
We believe in the Church, God's living grammar of grace,
Still speaking, still becoming,
Still echoing the joy of the world to come.

The future of doctrine is not a system of control but a song of faith, a melody of hope that leans forward into God's coming future. It is not confined to preservation, but composed in anticipation, shaped by the risen Christ, whose triumph over death assures us that love will have the final word, a song carried forward by the Spirit, echoing toward the renewal of all things, a Church that embodies doctrine as its living confession of faith.

As the Church walks forward into the world, the grammar of doctrine must be embodied in the witness of love.

And so, the Church hopes: Not in nostalgia, but in New Creation. Not in mastery, but in mercy. Not in certainty, but in communion. We believe that the infinite vulnerable Love that is God will outlast the grave, that the Spirit will teach us to sing again, and that doctrine, like breath, will rise with joy in every tongue, toward the Light of God's tomorrow.

Chapter Three
Doctrine Embodied
The Church as the Living Confession of Faith

From Communion to Creed

Doctrine arises from the shared life of love, not as its precondition but as its expression, challenging any account that would treat doctrine as a set of prior propositions. It is love that precedes and generates the need for articulation. In this sense, doctrine is not a gateway to belonging, but the language born from it, a language forged in communion, not in abstraction. Doctrine is a living witness to the faith and faithfulness of Christ, expressed through the Church's communal practices and sustained in its habits of grace.

We do not speak to belong. We speak because we already belong. In the economy of God's love, communion precedes confession. The fire of divine love descends not as a reward for right belief, as Pentecost so vividly reveals, but as the generative presence that creates the very possibility of faith. From this holy communion, *koinonia*, we are drawn together, awakened, and gathered into the shared life of God. And only then, as love takes root in us, do we find ourselves needing language to express what has already been made real.

This is the true order of knowing and loving in the Church: from fellowship to faith, from belonging to belief, from communion to creed, a sequence that embodies the very logic of this chapter's title, "Doctrine Embodied." It affirms that the Church's doctrinal confession is not first an intellectual assent, but a lived response to grace already received and shared. The great temptation of institutional Christianity has always been to reverse this flow, to insist that confession must come first, that right doctrine is the ticket to belonging. But this is not how the early Church was formed. Nor is it how the Spirit works.

The earliest creeds were not devised as gatekeeping instruments but as responses to grace, and they continue to offer the Church a model of doctrinal witness grounded in lived communion and sustained by the Spirit, a living confession that the Church must still embody today, formed within the life of a people who had encountered the risen Christ. They emerged from within worshiping, praying, suffering communities, those baptized in water, fire, and Spirit. The rule of faith, as it circulated in the second and third centuries, was passed on not through systematic debate but through the liturgical life and mission of the Church. Oorthodox tradition was shaped not only in polemic but in the lived memory of prayerful people who knew the truth of the gospel because they had experienced its love. This is the pattern of truth that follows the saving logic of the Gospel, the pattern by which love precedes knowledge, grace precedes formulation, and doctrine flows from the Spirit's transforming work in the life of the Church.

Early Christian doctrinal formation occurred through baptismal rites, catechesis, and eucharistic prayers, rather than imposed formulas. In this way, creeds did not create the Church's unity, they named it. The Church was already bound together by the Spirit who poured the love of God into their hearts. And in time, the people of God began to speak: We confess in the Creeds that "We believe in one God…," not to establish a formula of acceptance and belonging, but to express the love that was already burning among them.

The Apostles' Creed, the Nicene Creed, and even the early baptismal confessions were born from this kind of Triune love-soaked communion. The early Christian creeds arose organically as ways to shape memory and sustain unity, not to replace mystery with control, but to preserve it in shared language. The creeds gave voice to a communion already alive with grace. The real contagion was communion and fellowship with God and one another, and the language of faith expressed in their doctrines and creeds was forged to keep that fire of unitive love burning in those friendships with God and one another, for the life of the world.

This dynamic of friendship and belonging finds one of its earliest and most powerful expressions Irenaeus' affirmation that the glory of God is the human being fully alive in communion with God in what is perhaps the earliest Christian creed: "There is no longer Jew or Greek, slave or free, male and female; for all of you are one in Christ Jesus" (Gal. 3:28). At its heart, this is not a metaphysical proposition but a confession of radical belonging. It echoes the prayer of the Great High Priest for the unity of God's people (John 17), revealing that the earliest Christian creed was already shaped by communion and rooted in prayer. Such a confession arises not from abstract speculation but from the lived experience of the Spirit poured out on all flesh. It is the voice of a Church awakened to a new reality, the unity of all things in Christ, even amid radical difference. In this way, the Church's earliest doctrinal witness is not a system of ideas but a Spirit-breathed proclamation of love: all belong, all are one, all are held together in the reconciling life of Christ.

To reverse this, to require creed before communion, is to violate the very logic of grace. It is to treat love as conditional and belonging as transactional. But the Church is born at Pentecost, not at Nicea. It is the fire of the Spirit, not the precision of our formulations, that gathers the people of God and gives birth to faith.

Tradition lives only when it remains faithful to its origin, not simply as memory, but as embodiment. We must draw careful distinctions between tradition that gives life and traditionalism that deadens it. A living tradition becomes what Jaroslav Pelikan calls "the living faith of the dead" when it is continually rekindled in the fire of love. We must embrace a third image: tradition as an icon, a window into the mystery of God. In this sense, the Church's tradition is not merely a memory of doctrine, it is a living means of grace, an instrument through which the faithful encounter the mystery of Christ in the power of the Spirit. This reinforces the chapter's claim that doctrine, like tradition, must be born in communion and shaped by the Spirit's ongoing work in the life of the Church. This kind of tradition begins in communion, and it always overflows into doxology.

This is why John Wesley could insist on the ontological priority of love in all things. For Wesley, the Holy Spirit is the divine agent who awakens, nurtures, and perfects love within the believer and the Church. His pneumatology centers on the Spirit's transformative presence, which empowers the faithful to embody the love of God through concrete acts of grace, holiness, and communion. This Spirit-shaped love is not peripheral to doctrine, it is its heart. His famous phrase, "if your heart is as my heart, give me your hand," was not a rejection of doctrine, but a recognition that right belief is only right when it flows from right love. Wesley's doctrine was always relational, always situated in the life of the Church. Belief mattered, but only as a way to deepen the communion that God had already begun.

In the Wesleyan imagination, then, doctrine must never outpace grace. The Church does not confess faith in order to create unity. The Church confesses because she already shares in the life of the Triune God, the God who is communion, and whose love is the fire from which every creed must be spoken.

Doctrine in Practice
The Means of Grace

Doctrine lives when it is practiced in the rhythms of grace and the fellowship of the Church, when it is embodied as the Church's living confession, formed not merely in words but in shared practices of love and communion. In this way, doctrine becomes the Church's way of bearing witness to grace already received, it is embodied as the Church's vocation to be the Church's embodied witness to the faithfulness of Christ's love.

Doctrine is not only something the Church believes, it is something the Church does. This embodied practice of doctrine reinforces the chapter's central claim: that doctrine lives not in abstraction, but in the faithful enactment of the Church's shared life. It is lived, breathed, prayed, and practiced in the life of the body. The truths the Church confesses are not suspended in abstraction; they are grounded in worship, sustained in prayer, embodied in sacraments, and carried out in service. Doctrine is most faithful when it participates in the very life it proclaims: the Triune life of God poured out in love.

This is why John Wesley located the heart of theology not in scholastic speculation but in what he called the means of grace. For Wesley, these means were not simply devotional exercises, but Spirit-filled encounters that formed the Church's life and witness. Through the Spirit's active presence, these practices became instruments of sanctification and communal formation, embodying the grammar of divine love in action and shaping the Church's doctrinal life through lived encounter, shared grace, and responsive faith, shaping both the doctrine the Church proclaimed and the love it embodied. These were the ordinary channels through which God's love is received, responded to, and returned in prayer, searching the Scriptures, the Lord's Supper, fasting, Christian conferencing, and acts of mercy. Doctrine, for Wesley, was not theory to be debated, but grace to be encountered. If it could not be prayed, sung, or lived in love, it needed to be reformed.

In this way, the Church's teaching is inseparable from the Church's practice. To proclaim that Christ is risen is to gather at the Table. To confess the Trinity is to live in communion, to baptize in the name of Father, Son, and Spirit, to bless and be blessed in relationship. Doctrine is enacted as a doctrinal practice each time we forgive as we have been forgiven, or bear one another's burdens, a vision echoed by Augustine, who wrote that 'faith works through love' (Gal. 5:6), reminding us that doctrine, rightly lived, always expresses itself in acts of charity and reconciliation. It is performed in doxology. It is enfleshed in mission.

As William J. Abraham has emphasized in his recovery of the canonical heritage of the Church, the means of grace are not peripheral to theology, they are its source and structure. The canon is not only Scripture, but the sacramental, liturgical, communal, and spiritual life of the Church through which Christ is made present. Doctrine arises from this life and must return to it.

The Wesleyan tradition embodies this integrative vision by demonstrating that doctrine is not merely taught but practiced, embodied in the Church's lived confession of Christ's faithfulness through Spirit-led community, sacramental life, and acts of mercy. In doing so, it offers a corrective to modern tendencies that reduce doctrine to abstract systems or privatized belief. Instead, it situates doctrine within the Spirit-led practices of a communal life shaped by grace, showing that theological truth must be embodied, relational, and transformative. Its theology is not only about grace, but grace in motion. The Church gathers not simply to affirm ideas, but to be shaped by love, to be caught up again and again into the rhythm of God's self-giving. Wesley believed that all of God's commands are clothed in God's promises; so too are the doctrines of the Church when they embody the Faith of Christ that is filled with the energy of God's love. Each one is an invitation to grace, a summons to communion, a call to walk in love.

When doctrine is disconnected from these practices, it grows rigid and brittle. But when it flows within the life of the Church, through Eucharist and song, Scripture and service, reconciliation and prayer, it becomes a fire that forms and reforms us. It becomes what it was always meant to be: a means of grace, an embodied expression of the Church's living confession, shaped by love and sustained in the Spirit.

In this light, we might say that doctrine is not a conclusion, but a consecration, an embodied expression of the Church's identity as the living confession of the faith and faithfulness of Christ. It sets apart not just truths but lives. It marks the people of God as a community called not simply to believe in love, but to practice it, until every act of worship, every sharing of bread, every work of mercy becomes itself a confession: Christ is risen. The Spirit is here. And God is love.

Formation Through Habits of Faith

Doctrine becomes durable when it is shaped in the rhythms of grace and learned in the life of the Church, when it is embodied through practice, nourished in worship, and lived in communion. This durability arises not from rigidity but from being rooted in grace and sustained through the Church's life together.

Doctrine does not form us all at once. It takes root in repetition, relationship, and faithful practice, embodied realities through which the Church becomes the living confession of the faith and faithfulness of Christ. This is why the Church has always been more than a confessing community, it is a school of love, a body in formation. In the Wesleyan tradition, doctrine is not imposed as a fixed formula but cultivated in the habits of faith, unlike traditions that prioritize intellectual assent as the measure of orthodoxy. Wesley's approach offers a corrective: doctrine is formed not by coercion but through practices of shared grace, where belief is shaped within relationships of trust, prayer, and love. that arise through shared prayer, praise, and discipleship.

John Wesley understood this clearly. His model of Christian formation, through class meetings, band meetings, and societies, was rooted in the conviction that faith must be nurtured communally. Belief grows in proximity to others, where we learn to pray together, repent together, bear one another's burdens, and rejoice in grace. In these spaces, doctrine is not first about intellectual mastery; it is about shared trust. And it is this trust that gives rise to language.

Here the hymns of Charles Wesley become particularly powerful. They were not merely inspirational poetry but theological confession. In song, the people of God received doctrine not as dry abstraction, but as lived reality. They sang themselves into faith. As Wesley's hymns echoed through sanctuaries and class meetings, they formed hearts and minds alike. The theology they carried was born of prayer and returned to praise, a doxological rhythm that made their doctrine not only formative but transformative in the life of the Church.

The early Church Fathers knew this rhythm well. Athanasius, for instance, proclaimed the incarnation as the means by which humanity is drawn into the life of God, while Cyril of Jerusalem's catechetical lectures wove doctrinal instruction into liturgical and sacramental participation, both embodying doctrine as formation through worship and relationship. Patristic theology was never a detached exercise in speculation. It was always an act of reverence. Their doctrines were often forged in the midst of prayer, persecution, and the Eucharist. They spoke of the Trinity not as a philosophical puzzle, but as the name of the God they worshipped, encountered, and adored.

Doctrine, in this light, is not merely information, it is formation in the grammar of love, a shaping of life and community in the language that embodies Christ's faithfulness. It is catechesis through communion, theology through trust, memory shaped in love. The Church does not simply pass on ideas; it passes on a way of life. Through daily habits of prayer, works of mercy, communal discernment, and sacramental worship, the people of God are formed in faith and transformed by grace. As Vladimir Lossky explained, "We are becoming by God's grace what God is by nature."

Wesley clearly believed that the grace and wisdom found in the means of grace was the inhabiting presence of God. Athanasius, for instance, proclaimed the incarnation as the means by which humanity is drawn into the life of God, while Cyril of Jerusalem's catechetical lectures wove doctrinal instruction into liturgical and sacramental participation, both embodying doctrine as formation through worship and relationship. To participate in these means of grace is to partake of God. To use these means of grace we become as loving by God's grace as God is loving by nature. To practice the means of grace is to practice the love that is God.

This is why Wesley insisted that the means of grace must be practiced with constancy and joy, not to earn God's favor, but to remain open to it. As faith becomes habit, and habit becomes character, the Church becomes what it believes. It is not formed in isolation but through shared repetition, prayers said around the same table, hymns sung in harmony, bread broken in blessing. This is how faith becomes flesh.

In this communal life, doctrine is learned not simply by hearing, but by doing. Through these embodied acts of faith, the Church reveals herself as the living confession of the faith and faithfulness of Christ. It is learned when we forgive, when we confess, when we bless and are blessed. It is spoken in how we show up, in how we remember, in how we hope. This is the slow, faithful work of God's Spirit, to make us fluent in the language of love, until doctrine becomes not only something we profess, but something we embody.

Correcting Through Communion

Doctrine is preserved not by rigidity but by relationship, faithfully corrected through love.

Doctrine is not static. It is not a fossil from the past but a fire still burning in the present, a fire that echoes the Pentecost flame, kindled by the Spirit, which continues to ignite the Church's faith and illuminate her path through communion, love, and worship. A fire sustained and tended through the Church's communal life, worship, and shared practices of grace. In this way, doctrine remains a living flame that both illuminates and transforms the Church as the embodied confession of Christ's faithfulness. And like any living fire, it must be tended. This means doctrine must be corrected. But correction in the Church does not come through coercion or control. It comes through communion.

From the earliest days of the Church, theology was forged in conversation, in councils and synods, in letters and confessions, in tears and prayer. Even heresy, as H.E.W. Turner noted, plays a role in clarifying orthodoxy, not through exclusion alone, but through deeper discernment. When held in love, disagreement becomes a means of grace. These are like "silent orthodoxies," unspoken or hidden truths that are eclipsed because of our failure to see from a wider lens of love. Yet throughout history, the Church has rediscovered such truths when the Spirit opens our eyes anew, whether in reclaiming the dignity of women, affirming the unity of all believers across racial and cultural divides, or renewing the centrality of grace over legalism. These moments show that forgotten or eclipsed truths can be recovered when communion is prioritized over control. These "silent orthodoxies" hold potential to show us where the "heresies of love" are in our doctrines. The Church corrects its doctrine not to win arguments, but to bear more faithful witness to the love of God.

Heresies are like "silent orthodoxies" that can show us where the "heresies of love" are in our doctrines, those distortions of teaching that, while perhaps doctrinally precise, fail to reflect or nurture the radical love at the heart of the Gospel. The silent orthodoxies of love, these are places where truth has been severed from grace, and where communion must call doctrine back to its center in Christ's self-giving love. The Church corrects its doctrine not to win arguments, but to bear more faithful witness to the love of God.

John Wesley understood that doctrine must be tested by its fruits. His question did not stop with: "Is it true?" but "Does it lead to holiness? Does it increase love?" If some teaching harmed communion or obscured grace, it needed reform. Wesley's doctrine was shaped by love, not locked into polemic. His conferences and societies were places of mutual correction, holy listening spaces where trust permitted truth to surface.

This is the mark of living tradition: it does not enshrine the past but engages it, allowing the Church to continue embodying doctrine as its ongoing confession of Christ's faithful love in the present. It listens to the voices of the faithful, past and present, and asks what love requires today. Tradition lives only when it remains responsive to the Spirit. When doctrine ceases to grow in knowledge of love, it ceases to serve and harms the Body.

This is why doctrinal debates in the Church must be grounded in doxology and humility. The early Church exemplified this at the Council of Jerusalem (Acts 15), where leaders discerned truth together through prayerful dialogue, and again at Nicea, where creedal clarity would eventually emerge after a prolonged debate driven by political and cultural and theological differences and perspectives. Despite many coercive influences, both inside and outside the Church, it was through a deeper listening and discernment from the Spirit in shared worship and theological communion that produced the Church's confessed Faith through the Nicene Creed. We do not guard the truth by shouting louder or drawing sharper lines. We guard it by listening, confessing, forgiving, and walking in love. As the Church gathers around the Table, it becomes a place not only of communion, but of correction, a community that believes enough to be vulnerable, to be refined.

The distinction between correction and fulfillment is vital. Correction is not the abandonment of doctrinal inheritance but its ongoing fulfillment, removing distortions along the way that obscure the heart of the gospel. Fulfillment, by contrast, is the unfolding of that inheritance in new ways that respond to fresh insight or need, much like the early Church's fuller understanding of the Trinity emerged in response to Christological questions. Together, they ensure that doctrine remains both faithful to the telos of its origins and faithfully open to the Spirit's ongoing revelation to fulfill the end goal of God's promise. The goal is not to undo or delete the faith that came before, but to let the faith of the past breathe in the present, to correct what inhibits God's promise, and to fulfill what love still yearns to express. Doctrine becomes faithful when it remains porous to grace and always open to God's future and ours in the promise of New Creation.

Doctrine is not maintained by building walls; it is nurtured by building trust, trust grounded in communion, sustained through shared practices of grace, and embodied in the Church's living confession of Christ's faithfulness. In this way, the Church becomes again what she is always called to be: the living confession of the faith and faithfulness of Christ, bearing witness to the love that holds all things together for the life of the world. This is the work of communion. It is slow, relational, and Spirit-led. But it is the only way doctrine can remain what it is meant to be: the Church's witness to the love that holds all things together.

A Belonging That Believes

Flowing directly from the Church's commitment to correction in communion, faith is not the prerequisite to belonging but its fruit; doctrine gives language to the love we already share. It is the embodied confession of a Church already gathered into the life of Christ by the Spirit.

We do not believe in order to belong; we believe because we have already been drawn into love. It is not assent that earns us a place, but communion that teaches us to speak. This is the truth that pulses through the earliest creeds of the Church and echoes in the Spirit's work from Pentecost to today. Belonging precedes belief, and doctrine is the language we learn to speak in the household of God's love. In the Church, we do not earn our place by what we profess. We profess our faith because we have already been given a place at the Table.

The deepest truths of Christian doctrine are confessions of relationship. When we say, "I believe," we are saying not merely that we assent to a proposition, but that we trust a Person, and that we do so with others. Doctrine is communal grammar. It is the shared language of a people who are learning to love what God loves, and to see each other as beloved.

This is why Stephen J. Patterson and others identify Galatians 3:28 as a foundational creed: "There is no longer Jew or Greek, slave or free, male and female, for all are one in Christ Jesus." It is not a statement of speculative theology; it is a declaration of unity. It names a belonging already secured by the Spirit. And it is this communal reality that makes belief possible.

In the Wesleyan tradition, this is echoed in the way faith is formed through band meetings, class meetings, and the embodied life of the Church. Doctrine must never become untethered from the Church; it must always grow within it, as a dynamic communion of love shaped by the Spirit and grounded in the relational vision at the heart of Wesleyan theology. Far from being abstract formulations imposed from above, doctrine for Wesley arises within the shared practices of grace and is sustained by the Spirit's presence in community. This rooting in communal life keeps doctrine vibrant, accountable, and transformative. Wesley understood that people come to faith not just through teaching, but through testimony. Through being welcomed. Through being prayed for. Through seeing love enacted. In short, through belonging.

The practices of worship, Scripture, sacraments, and spiritual discipline are not mechanisms of gatekeeping; they are the soil in which faith grows. Doctrine is a fruit of this life, not a fence to protect it. Too often, doctrine has been weaponized as a means of exclusion. The question has been framed: "What must you believe to belong here?" But the gospel flips this question on its head: "Because you already belong, what might you now dare to believe?"

Hospitality, as envisioned by theologians like the distinguished Lettey M. Russell, is not a peripheral ethic but a doctrinal act, a practice through which the Church embodies and performs its confession of God's faithful love in the world. Hospitality is not simply social but theological, a practice that forms the Church as a living confession of God's faithfulness through inclusive, grace-filled relationships that resonates with this inversion. We must dismantle rigid ecclesial structures and instead center the Church's identity on hospitality, a radically inclusive welcome as the foundation for all theological reflection and communal life. The Church's identity is not grounded in a hierarchy of correct belief and episcopal control but expressed as a table of shared grace, embodying doctrine through inclusive community and mutual hospitality where doctrine is shaped through mutual service and loving presence.

Belonging is not earned. It is revealed by the Spirit, who draws us into communion with God and one another. It is the grace that opens our ears to hear the Word, that opens our hearts to receive the Spirit, that opens our mouths to speak what we know to be true: that God is love, and that we are loved.

Doctrine must be forged in community, not merely handed down in isolation, it must be shaped through shared worship, sacramental life, acts of mercy, and mutual service, where the Church's confession is continually formed by love embodied in practice. When we believe together, we do so in the context of mutual love, vulnerability, and trust. Faith that is born in belonging does not need to dominate or divide. It needs only to witness, to tell the truth about the love that found us first.

In the end, the grammar of doctrine is simply this: We belong. We believe. We are becoming. This is the work of the

Spirit forming us in love, not alone, but together. In Christ. By the Spirit. For the glory of God and the life of the world.

Faith and Doctrine in the Church's Future

The Church speaks doctrine in the voice of love, not to control the future, but to welcome it in trust and hope.

Flowing from the rhythm of belonging, believing, and becoming, doctrine is not about securing permanence for faith, it is the Church's embodied confession of the faith and faithfulness of Christ, carried forward as living testimony into God's future. It is about witnessing to the infinite vulnerable love of God that is from everlasting to everlasting. As the Church moves into an uncertain future, albeit a future filled with hope and promise, doctrine must not become a relic we defend, but a living testimony we continue to speak, in humility, in faith, and in love. What abides is not the form of our words but the Spirit who breathes through them.

The future of doctrine depends on its willingness to remain open to the Spirit, the same Spirit who, at Pentecost, set hearts ablaze and gave the Church a new tongue of love and witness. Doctrine must stay open because the Spirit is always speaking anew, always leading the Church deeper into God's vulnerable, transforming love. This does not mean forgetting our past. It means listening to it with deeper reverence and greater trust. It means discerning what the Spirit is saying now, in light of what has been faithfully said before. Doctrine must never be frozen in time. It must remain in motion, carried by the life of the Church as it grows into the love of God.

John Wesley captured this vision when he insisted that the Church must be "going on to perfection," not merely toward personal holiness, but toward deeper participation in the Triune life of God. Christian perfection is not the end of striving, but the ever-deepening communion with God that doctrine must serve, form, and express. simply toward a personal or ecclesial ideal, but toward a future grammar of doctrine shaped in communion and transformation, not toward a finished system of thought, but toward a more perfect love. Doctrine is not static knowledge; it is infinite love that is always expanding and thus our doctrines are always seeking a new grammar of faith and understanding for the journey. It is the unfolding articulation of the Church's journey into God. It must always be shaped by prayer, by communion, by suffering, and by joy.

Doctrine, especially Trinitarian doctrine, is never an abstract framework imposed upon divine mystery, but a doxological expression of the God who comes to us in love. Catherine LaCugna's superb book, *God for Us* taught us that theology must always serve communion, it must arise from the life of the Church and return to it. Doctrine that is future-oriented is also relational, formed in the shared vulnerability of being drawn into the life of God.

The Church's confession is never about escape from history but participation in God's redemptive future. The resurrection of Jesus is not only the hinge of history but the source of our hope. The Church, by its very life, bears witness to the coming renewal of all things. Thus, doctrine is not merely retrospective; it is anticipatory. It reaches forward in hope, carrying the memory of God's faithfulness into the promise of New Creation.

The fire of God's love that formed the early creeds must be the same fire that forms our witness today. Doctrine must be spoken from that fire, or not at all. For it is the Spirit who kindles this fire, who animates the Church's witness, and who continues to speak through doctrine when it arises from communion, prayer, and love. If it is not born in prayer, animated by love, and hospitable to hope, then it ceases to serve. Doctrine that does not bless cannot believe. It becomes brittle, and the world rightly turns away.

But there is another way. Doctrine can welcome the future as gift. It can become the Church's poetry of love, testifying to grace with language that is both ancient and new. When doctrine is rooted in communion, it is free to speak boldly and gently, prophetically and pastorally. It can learn new dialects. It can sing new songs.

The Church's witness will remain credible not because it controls the culture, but because it continues to love. Doctrine will endure not because it is enforced, but because it is embodied in lives of holiness, hospitality, and hope, lives that together bear witness to the Church's vocation as the living confession of the faith and faithfulness of Christ. The Church proclaims and embodies the Good News of Christ for the life of the world.

This is why the work of doctrine must remain tethered to prayer, shaped in community, and fired by the imagination of the Spirit. Only then can it speak with a voice that still sounds like good news. The Church does not speak faithful doctrine as the grammar of God's love to possess the truth, but to be possessed by it, to be caught up again and again in the mystery of Christ, the Word made flesh.

As we look to the future, we must teach doctrine not as law, but as love. We must write it not only in books, but in lives, lives shaped by the Spirit's ongoing work through the Church's communal practices of prayer, worship, and love. And we must confess it not to preserve the past, but to prepare the way for God's promised New Creation. This is how doctrine becomes hope.

And this is how the Church becomes what she believes: the living Body of Christ, speaking the Word in the language of love.

Confession of the Church's Future Faith
We believe in love that cannot die.
We believe in Christ, risen and interceding.
We believe in the Spirit, who breathes through our doctrine and forms our hope.
We believe the Church is the living breathing Body of Christ, called to embody Christ's faith, proclaim the Good News and love with the love that is the infinite vulnerable love of God, and welcome God's future.

Mandate of Embodied Doctrine
Therefore, let us teach doctrine as love.
Let us confess not to control, but to serve.
Let us write theology with our lives.
Let us go forth, to become what we believe,
to speak what we have received,
and to live what we confess:

that Christ is risen,
the Spirit is here,
and God is love.

Chapter Four
Doctrine Remembered
The Story That Shapes the Church

"Do this in remembrance of me."
Luke 22:19
"Tradition is the living faith of the dead; traditionalism is the dead faith of the living."
Jaroslav Pelikan

Tradition as Memory in Motion

At the close of Chapter 3, we witnessed how the Church, as the embodied confession of faith, bears doctrine not as rigid proposition but as a Spirit-given testimony of love lived in communion. Chapter 4 now turns to explore how this confession is also a memory, alive, hopeful, and transformative. Doctrine, as remembered truth, is not a relic but a rhythm, a theological and liturgical pattern that pulses through the life of the Church, shaped by memory, sustained by the Spirit, and oriented toward God's promised future: a Spirit-breathed inheritance that links past, present, and future. This chapter unfolds how tradition becomes the grammar through which the Church remembers in love, is corrected in love, and is carried forward by love toward New Creation.

Tradition lives when it breathes with the Spirit who draws the promised future into the Church's present. The memory of the Church is not a backward glance, but a Spirit-animated witness to the continuity of God's redeeming action across time. Because the Spirit is the Lord of time, brooding over creation, descending at Pentecost, and leading all things to fulfillment in Christ, tradition becomes a pneumatological mediation of past, present, and future. It is memory in motion. Living tradition is not the past preserved but the past transfigured in the present by the Spirit's inbreaking of the promised future, a future that gives tradition its shape as the grammar of divine love, spoken by the Church in every age as a Spirit-breathed response to God's faithfulness. When tradition cuts itself off from the novelty of the Spirit, it calcifies into traditionalism, what Jaroslav Pelikan calls "the dead faith of the living." But when it breathes with the energy of love, tradition recalls not only where we have been, but where God is taking us. It becomes the flame of love rather than the fossil of habit.

This flame is kindled most vividly at the Table. Christ's command, "Do this in remembrance of me," is not nostalgia but eschatological invocation. In the Eucharist, this remembering is more than mental recall, it is anamnesis, a doctrinal act in which memory, hope, and communal identity are fused. Here, the Church enters the mystery of Christ's presence, bearing witness to the faithfulness of God by re-membering the Body in love, in time, and in anticipation of New Creation. At the Table, the Church remembers in the present her past, and she remembers in anticipation of her future. The Eucharist is anamnesis, sacramental memory that re-members the Body and reconstitutes the world. It is a divine act of remembering that reconnects and reorders all things in Christ: what has been broken, excluded, or rendered obsolete is gathered into God's future. In the promise of God, nothing is discarded. In the breath of God, even dry bones live again.

Ezekiel's vision of the valley of dry bones (Ezekiel 37) captures this re-membering. The Spirit breathes life into forgotten fragments, raising them into communion. The Spirit re-members the house of Israel, raising, restoring, reanimating. Likewise, the Church's memory is not a passive recollection, but an act of resurrection: a calling forth of life from what appears forgotten. To remember is a living act of faith, love, and eschatological imagination. Memory becomes an anticipatory participation in New Creation.

This is the rhythm of Spirit-breathed tradition. It remembers not to preserve, but to transform. Tradition lives when it breathes deeply with the breath of the Spirit. John Wesley's vision of the Church as the "new habitation of God in the Spirit" reflects this same dynamic. The Church, for Wesley, is a community of promise where doctrine, prayer, and mission arise from communion with the divine life. Memory, when animated by the Spirit, becomes a participation in the future glory already begun.

Tradition is best understood not as a static inheritance but as the Spirit's ongoing act of interpretation, an act sustained through the Church's attention to Scripture, sacrament, and silence. This habit of attention is itself a kind of grammar of love, shaped across time by the Spirit's faithful witness. It reinforces that doctrinal memory is not passive recall but active, Spirit-led participation in God's unfolding promise. Tradition is the Church's Spirit-formed habit of attention, its prayerful discernment of God's voice across time, shaped by Scripture, silence, and sacramental encounter. Together, attentive memory and future vision frame doctrine not as a static archive but as a dynamic orientation toward the inbreaking of newness, doctrine remembered in the Spirit, not for preservation alone but as a grammar of love that breathes toward God's future. Tradition is the Church's Spirit-formed habit of attention, its prayerful discernment of God's voice across time, shaped by Scripture, silence, and sacramental encounter.

Tradition, then, is not an anchor dragging us back but a sail catching the wind of the Spirit, a sail shaped by Eucharistic memory and lifted by eschatological hope, drawing the Church forward with the Spirit's breath into God's unfolding future. This image echoes the chapter's arc, where the Spirit breathes through memory, correction, fulfillment, and embodiment, drawing the Church into the wide horizon of God's promised future. This sail is set by the winds of God's future, hope shaping memory. The sail is held steady by prayerful attention and contemplative discernment and oriented toward reconciliation, healing, and hospitality.

Tradition then speaks with a grammar of love shaped in time, always being re-spoken by the Spirit who animates the Church's life in the present and draws it toward the fullness of Christ. It grounds us in God's faithfulness yet propels us toward new expressions of love that are still unfolding. "The faith once delivered to the saints" remains constant in love, but its language, forms, and possibilities keep expanding as the Spirit who is the energy of God's infinite vulnerable love continues to speak and sing creation into newness.

Tradition and the Spirit of Correction

If tradition is a memory in motion, then it must also be a memory willing to be reformed, a sail, not an anchor, open to the wind of the Spirit who draws the Church forward. As we move from memory into correction, the same Spirit who re-members the Body now renews its witness. This section moves from the beauty of living memory to its vulnerability: tradition must remain open to the Spirit's correction. The doctrine we inherit is not above refinement, it is shaped and reshaped by the love that calls it into deeper fidelity. Here, the Church listens for the voice that still speaks, trusting that divine love not only remembers but renews.

Tradition is alive when it yields to the Spirit's work of correction, refinement, and sanctification. Correction is not rejection of the tradition but deepened faithfulness. As seen in the Church's historic affirmations: such as the refinement of Christological doctrine between Nicaea and Chalcedon, correction often emerges from listening more carefully to the gospel and more faithfully to the Spirit. In such moments, the Church doesn't abandon its inheritance but seeks to bear truer witness to it by letting go of that which "now" hinders the fulfillment of the inbreaking future of God's promise. If doctrine is the Church's grammar of faith and love, then the ongoing correction of doctrine is the continual work of love. This is how the Spirit prunes and renews the Church so that tradition may more clearly bear witness to Christ and move more faithfully forward into the infinite vulnerable love that never ends.

Just as individuals are sanctified by grace, so too is the Church's shared confession of faith. Correction is the Spirit's discipline for love's sake. When tradition resists correction, it ossifies and dies. But when it remains open and vulnerable to the Spirit's voice, it is reformed in joy and fidelity by the perfect love that is God.

This the dual movement of what Pelikan caslls "correction and fulfillment" is a Spirit-led dynamic that sustains apostolic continuity while unfolding new expressions of love; it ensures that doctrine remains both rooted and responsive: rooted in the faith once delivered, yet responsive to the Spirit who corrects, renews, and fulfills tradition in light of God's ongoing self-disclosure. The Spirit ensures both the continuity of apostolic faith and its transformation in love. Correction is not merely doctrinal adjustment but the Spirit's gracious initiative to bring tradition into deeper alignment with the unfolding mystery of Christ. Fulfillment, then, is not completion as closure, but fulfillment as deeper participation in the divine life that continually renews the Church. The early Church understood this deeply.

The great councils of Nicaea, Constantinople, and Chalcedon were not merely doctrinal battlegrounds or political necessities. They were prayerful, painful efforts to bear faithful witness to the mystery of God. We are possessed by truth, and thus, participate in it through faith, hope and love. Our doctrines are provisional, not because truth is unstable, but because the irruption of God's future into ours is always changing our way of seeing through faith, hope and love. God's promise is not a fixed archive but a future that is still arriving. The Spirit continues to lead us into all truth (John 16:13), not as an endpoint but as a pilgrimage into ever deeper participation in Christ. As we look over the horizon and see the future of God coming to us, we do not see the finish of all but the beginning of all truth that is as infinite as the infinite vulnerable love that is God.

Tradition and the Fulfillment of Promise

If correction opens tradition to its sanctifying renewal, like fire purifying and breath reviving, then fulfillment draws it toward its radiant end, carried still by the Spirit's forward-moving grace. From pruning to flowering, the grammar of doctrine must be shaped not only by what has been received, but by what God has promised to complete. Section 3 now turns from correction to consummation, from the Spirit's refining fire to the horizon of love's full arrival. The Church, formed in memory, moves now toward maturity in hope.

Tradition lives when it opens itself to the future it confesses: the fulfillment of God's love. Christian tradition is eschatological before it is historical. It is not merely a backward-looking memory, but a forward-leaning witness to the promises of God. Tradition bears the memory of divine faithfulness precisely because it trusts in the future that memory anticipates. In this way, tradition becomes a vessel of promise, a testimony that what God has begun will be brought to completion.

Tradition, then, is not a static deposit of unchanging truths, but a living current of love that flows toward its telos in Christ, carried in the words of liturgy, the rhythm of confession, and the faithful improvisation of lives rooted in grace and directed by hope. It remembers not only what has been said and done, but what has been promised and is still unfolding. It sings of what is yet to come.

John Henry Newman described tradition as organic development: a vision that resonates with the Church's forward movement toward fulfillment. His metaphor of growth, doctrine as a living organism, suggests not only continuity with the past but orientation toward the future. In this eschatological light, tradition grows not merely by accumulation but by reaching toward the fullness of love that God has promised. Doctrine grows like a living organism, rooted in Christ yet expanding as the Church reflects more deeply on the mystery it inhabits. Doctrine does not spring forth in full bloom, but grows in continuity with its source, like a tree from its seed, planted by the streams of living water, as Psalm 1 envisions, or as a branch abiding in the vine of John 15. This growth is nourished by prayer, contemplation, and faithful witness, stretching always toward the light of Christ. For Newman, heresy was not simply wrong belief but false innovation or a "heresy of love" that severs this growth from its source, the living breathing energy of God's love. True development, by contrast, remains anchored in the unchanging faithfulness of Christ, even as it expands in understanding and expression. The Church's speech about God must always stretch to meet the reality of the God who speaks first.

Doctrine is never static commentary but a Spirit-led response to Christ's living presence. Doctrinal development is the Church's contemplative and context-responsive maturation in faith, a living response that reinforces tradition as a movement toward fulfillment. Doctrinal growth is not a detour from the gospel but the unfolding of its meaning in ever new contexts, rooted in contemplation and responsive to the witness of holiness across time.

When doctrine is understood in this way, doctrinal fulfillment is not understood as speculative expansion, but as a Spirit-led deepening, rooted in the Church's prayerful receptivity to God's desire and love. Fulfillment does not come through theological invention but through prayer that listens to God's future pressing into the Church's present. True fulfillment is born in the silence where God's transformative love and desire takes root.

The earliest Christian communities confessed Jesus as Lord long before articulating the doctrines of the Trinity or Incarnation. But under the pressures of worship, persecution, and love, the Church's confession grew more precise, not to control mystery, but to honor it, not because it did not already experience the mystery of love, but because it knew that the inexhaustible mystery of infinite vulnerable love could never be contained. The Spirit did not preserve the Church in silence but gave it a voice for every age.

Still, fulfillment must not be confused with finality. Because the Spirit continues to speak and stir the Church, fulfillment remains a journey rather than a conclusion, an invitation into love that never ends and a grammar that is still being sung by the breath of God. Tradition remains open-ended because the Spirit who indwells the Church is always at work, always speaking anew. Fulfillment is thus not closure, but a widening of participation in the divine life, a love that continues to draw the Church deeper into mystery, hope, and communion. Tradition is fulfilled not when it is finished, but when it is transfigured, taken up into the ongoing life of God's promise. The love that is God is the source of our life and this love that is the source of the Church's grammar of faith is never finished. Doctrinal fulfillment is not the end of development but its deepening. Fulfillment does not abandon origin; it brings it to maturity.

For Wesley, sanctification was this dynamic fulfillment: the unfolding of grace into greater love. Salvation was not a moment to be claimed but a movement to be joined. The Church, as the Body of Christ, is called to cooperate with grace, not only to receive the promise but to participate in it. Doctrine grows in grace as it is enacted in lives conformed to Christ.

The Eucharist again becomes a sign of fulfillment, enacting both memory and promise in a single sacramental act, an extension of the anamnetic rhythm explored above. Just as Eucharistic memory fuses past and future in the Spirit's present action, so here the Table becomes the convergence of fulfilled promise and anticipated glory. In this act, the Church does not merely remember what was; she lives into what is coming. It gathers the Church's past and future into a present moment of communion, embodying the anamnetic rhythm explored in earlier chapters.

In this act, tradition does not merely recall, it anticipates, revealing the Table as the place where remembrance becomes hope and the promise of new creation is made tangible in the breaking of bread. In anamnesis, the Church remembers forward. The Table is not a static symbol but a sacramental act where promise becomes presence. As the liturgy is construed as a structured encounter with God it becomes a kind of tradition-in-motion: language and form handed down and lifted up, prayed anew by each generation. In Word and Sacrament, tradition fulfills its calling, to mediate the presence of the Risen Christ in the life of the Church.

Tradition's fulfillment is not finality, but transfiguration. Doctrine is taken up into the radiant life of Christ, where what was whispered becomes proclamation and what was seed becomes fruit. What was once hidden is revealed in the glory and love of God.

The Church as the Breathing Icon

If tradition fulfills its purpose in love's consummation, then it must take visible, embodied form. This section explores how that fulfillment becomes iconographic. Just as doctrine shapes memory and hope, it must also shape life, lived, seen, and shared. Here the Church is revealed as the breathing icon of the Triune God: a sacramental community whose form reflects the content of the love she proclaims.

To say the Church is an icon of the Triune God is to say she participates in who she proclaims, embodying, like tradition itself, a grammar of love made visible. Iconography, in this sense, becomes a theological language, a form of witness through which the Church speaks the mystery it inhabits. Christ, the image (*eikōn*) of the invisible God, becomes the measure and meaning of tradition. The Church, as Christ's Body, is called to bear that image, "to become by grace what God is by nature."

Icons are to the eyes what music is to the ears. Together, the icons of the East and the music of the West gesture beyond themselves, awakening a desire for what cannot be possessed but entered to participate in. Icons are not ends in themselves; they are means of grace to reach our end: as loving by God's grace as God is by nature.

Jaroslav Pelikan's typology (idol, token, icon) sharpens this distinction and deepens the Church's iconographic vocation. Avoiding idolatry means refusing to confuse the Church with God; avoiding tokenism means resisting reduction to cultural nostalgia or shallow symbolism. An icon, by contrast, is transparent to what it signifies, it points beyond itself to the Triune love it reflects. This clarity in distinction helps the Church understand her calling: to be a faithful, grace-filled window through which the self-giving love of God shines visibly in the world. An idol traps; a token forgets and thus misrepresents. But an icon is transparent to what it signifies. The Church, as the Body of Christ, shares in this iconographic vocation. She is called to be a visible, tangible, breathing sign of God's self-giving love. As such, the Church is not the source of light, but a window through which the light shines. She is the temple not of her own glory, but of the Spirit's indwelling presence.

The Church's identity is inherently participatory, a reality that shapes her iconographic calling. To be drawn into the kenotic pattern of divine love is not only to reflect God ethically but also to image God visually through cruciform existence. This participation makes the Church not just a witness to the gospel, but a living, breathing icon of the self-giving Christ in both form and action. To be justified is to be drawn into the kenotic shape of divine love, and to be Church is to inhabit this cruciform pattern publicly and communally. The Church does not merely proclaim the gospel; it becomes the gospel, a cruciform, Spirit-filled community whose very life is mission. This echoes the Wesleyan vision of holiness as shared life in love, a Spirit-enabled participation in Christ's self-giving for the world. The Church, then, as the icon of the crucified and risen Lord, embodies the divine life it proclaims, becoming by grace what Christ is by nature.

John Wesley's vision of the Church as the "new habitation of God in the Spirit" captures this beautifully. For Wesley, the Church was not simply the custodian of God's grace, but the place where that grace is embodied in real community. Holiness was not an individual achievement but a shared participation in divine love. The Church is a Spirit-animated body, not just a people who proclaim the gospel, but who become its visible form in the world. To become the Gospel for the life of the world is to partake of the very nature of the infinite vulnerable love that is God.

The Church breathes in the Spirit through prayer, Scripture, and sacrament, and breathes out that same Spirit through hospitality, justice, forgiveness, and joy. When the Church lives this rhythm, her tradition is not brittle but buoyant, not a relic but a vessel of life.

This is sacramental imagination in motion. In her liturgies, the Church does not simply remember Christ, she encounters him. In her doctrine, she does not merely recite truth, she bears it. In her community, she does not merely reflect the gospel, she becomes a foretaste of the kingdom.

This is the mystery of the Church as icon: she is what she proclaims.

To be faithful to tradition, then, is not to imprison it in yesterday's forms, but to offer it anew as a window through which the Spirit can breathe today. Icons are only faithful when they are transparent to what they signify. So too with tradition. It is only truly tradition when it points beyond itself, to Christ, to the Spirit, to the Father's everlasting love.

The Church, as the breathing icon of God's love, does not bear witness to her own greatness. She bears witness to the One who became flesh, who dwells among us still, and who is even now making all things new.

Remembering Forward, Tradition as Hope

Tradition's journey, from memory to correction to iconography, finds its pulse in hope, a hope already enacted in the Eucharist, where memory and promise converge. This sacramental rhythm, carried forward by the Spirit, anchors the Church's trust in the God who is making all things new. In this final section, the Church is called to remember not only what God has done, but to trust what God has promised. Hope transforms memory into mission, and doctrine into promise-bearing, a movement carried on the breath of the Spirit. Just as memory is animated by the Spirit's presence, so too is hope the forward-pulling energy of divine love that keeps the Church leaning into God's future. The Church remembers forward, living into the future by the Spirit's breath, animated by the love that is always arriving.

Tradition fulfills its purpose when it becomes a vessel of hope. It is the memory of God's faithfulness animated by trust in God's future. Eschatological hope is always prior to the historical past. Because the Spirit's presence is both remembrance and promise, memory becomes a participation in what shall be.

Christian hope is not optimism but trust in the character of the Promise-Giver. As Wesley observed, God's commands are always clothed in God's promises. It is not rooted in human progress, ingenuity, or positive thinking. It is anchored in the character of God, the God who raised Jesus from the dead and who will bring all things to completion. Hope, for the Church, is not an aspiration but participation in a promise already alive within us. This hope bears witness even amid suffering and delay, for it knows that the Spirit groans with us and for us as we await the redemption of all things.

Hope is the refusal to let the past determine the future; it is the resolve to live now by the peace that is promised. This reconciliatory vision not only restores relationship but echoes the Eucharistic promise: a foretaste of the eschatological banquet where enemies become guests and strangers become kin. In this way, reconciliation becomes sacramental, embodying the hope of a world made new. that Christian hope is always tied to reconciliation. Remembering forward means remembering faithfully, with an eye toward justice, forgiveness, and the embrace of enemies.

Tradition becomes hopeful when it leans into the promise, when it allows the Eucharist to embody the future it anticipates. In the breaking of bread and sharing of the cup, the Church enacts a memory that looks forward: an anamnetic act where sacramental memory fuses past and promise into a single present grace. This moment at the Table embodies the Church's theological rhythm, memory in motion, where doctrine is not only recalled but anticipated, making the Eucharist a forward-leaning expression of hope.

This is a sacrament that not only recalls Christ's self-giving love but also rehearses the joy and justice of the feast to come that it sees and tastes. This embodied hope nourishes the Church to risk speaking with a new grammar of love, to be broken, blessed, and given again, like the bread at the Table, as a foretaste of the banquet to come. In this light, tradition becomes sacramental, it risks new language, when it allows itself to be broken, blessed, and given again, like the bread at the Table, as a foretaste of the banquet to come. It does not merely preserve or defend the past; it trusts in the promise of God. And by the energy of divine love, it becomes the bread for the world, broken, blessed, and given again, as a sign of the Christ who is always coming.

The Church, as the body of Christ, is the place where memory and hope meet, where saints sing beside seekers, and the Spirit breathes new life into old bones. To remember forward is to follow in the Way of Jesus. As Jesus grew in wisdom and stature by trusting the Spirit, he became the Christ, the One who embodies the energy of God's love and shows us how to walk in trust and love. To remember forward is to carry the stories of the faithful into places they never imagined. It is to receive what has been handed down with gratitude, and to offer it again with the courage of love, the same love that raised our Lord from the grave. It is to trust the Spirit who descended at Pentecost and is still descending, still speaking, still forming a people of many tongues and many traditions, filled with the energy of love, for the life of the world.

Tradition will remain credible "only" if it remains hopeful. Only if it continues to confess Christ not as a relic but as a living presence. Only if it teaches the Church to remember, not in fear, but in faith. Not to defend the past, but to proclaim the promised future of New Creation. Not to build monuments to yesterday's certainties, but to become, even now, a foretaste of what shall be.

To remember forward is to hold past and future together in the present as gift. It is to walk in the Way of Christ, to sing old songs with new verses, to become what we proclaim. Tradition will remain credible only if it remains hopeful, only if it points not to itself, but to the risen and returning Christ.

For Jesus is the Christ who embodies the content and the fulfillment of every promise of God. He is the Alpha and the Omega, the One who goes before us and the One who calls us forward. The Church remembers forward because Christ leads us there. He is the song still being sung, the light still rising, the love that is always arriving.

To remember forward is to live now in light of what shall be: a Church transfigured by love, a world made new, and a song that rises from every tongue, tribe, and nation, echoing through time and beyond time, to the glory of God.

Tradition, then, is not a monument but a movement, a love-shaped memory carried forward by the Spirit, echoing the promise: "Behold, I make all things new."

Doctrine remembered is doctrine transfigured. This transfiguration is born from contemplative attentiveness to the Spirit's groaning. Doctrine matures through imaginative readiness for divine surprise.

Memory anchors us in the Spirit's faithfulness; correction purifies us in the fire of God's love; fulfillment stretches us toward the horizon of promise; embodiment makes love visible in the communion of the Church; and hope sings the song of what shall be. In all these, the Spirit shapes a faithful doctrine that breathes with the life of Christ's Faith and faithfulness, ever ancient and ever new testifying to the God who was, and is, and is to come.

May the Church remember forward, transfigured by love,
until all things speak with the language of grace and all creation
joins the song of God's future.
Amen.

Chapter Five
Doctrine Made Flesh
Formation for God's Future

"The Church changes the world not by making converts but by making disciples."
John Wesley
"Faith is not the work of isolated individuals, but the labor of a community formed by Word and Spirit, fashioned into Christ's likeness by love."
John Wesley

Doctrine is not only confessed and enacted; it is also taught, remembered, and lived over time. In this chapter, we explore doctrine as a spiritual pedagogy, an instrument of formation that cultivates faith, hope, and love in communities shaped by God's future. This formation happens not merely in academic spaces but in the relational, embodied, and communal life of the Church.

From Memory to Embodied Witness

If tradition is memory in motion, a remembering forward shaped by the Spirit's breath, then it resonates with the Church's eschatological identity. It calls the Church to live as a community that anticipates and embodies God's promised future even now: a community called to anticipate and embody God's promised future even now. The Church's memory is not merely retrospective but anticipatory. She remembers in order to embody the promises of God through present practices of love and witness. In this way, memory becomes an active posture of hope, linking the Church's historical rootedness to her vocation as a foretaste of New Creation. The Church does not merely think or speak tradition; she sings it, paints it, kneels in it, and consumes it. She remembers forward not only with her mind but with her senses, not only in doctrine but in doxology. The promise of New Creation is not a disembodied abstraction of eschatological hope, it is the transfiguration of our whole humanity and all things of creation into the life of God.

When doctrine breathes, it no longer rests solely on the creedal pages of the Church, it becomes music in the sanctuary, fragrance in the oil, icon on the walls, and bread on the tongues of those awakened in the living Body of Christ. The Church becomes not only the memory of God's past love but its living, breathing icon, as Eastern Orthodox theology suggests a visible sign of divine beauty and communion, transparent to the mystery it proclaims: namely, the self-giving love of the Triune God drawing all creation toward its consummation. Doctrine, in this light, is not a frozen articulation from the Church's dogma, but a dynamic expression that forms and transforms the Church's common life, shaping how communities embody grace, practice forgiveness, and live into God's future with hope and fidelity. Doctrine becomes the faithful grammar of divine love, a dynamic language that not only informs but also enacts the love it proclaims, shaping the Church's habits, relationships, and imagination. It cultivates not only theological clarity, but a way of life rooted in grace and directed toward God's future, a community formed not around mere ideas, but around the living presence of Christ. Faithful doctrine becomes a transfigured witness: memory carried forward in the breath of the Spirit, shaping a community of faith with the "hope of glory" already begun.

Such embodiment is not ornamental, it is formative. The Church's life becomes a spiritual pedagogy, where doctrine is not static but shapes disciples in habits of God's future. Doctrine is not an information dump in the form of theological propositions, as can sometimes occur in certain strands of scholasticism or classical fundamentalism; it is a formative discipline shaped by eschatological hope. It teaches not only what to believe, but how to see, desire, and act with the infinite vulnerable love that is God.

Philosopher James K. A. Smith provocatively asserts that we are not merely "brains on sticks" who think our way through the world, but fundamentally desiring creatures, liturgical beings whose loves are habituated through embodied practices. Liturgical anthropology like Smith's reinforces the Church's role as a communal and sensory pedagogical space. Doctrine, then, is not merely taught but embodied through rhythms of worship and shared life. Just as secular liturgies: such as those of the mall, stadium, or nation-state, form our desires through repeated symbolic practices and desires through repeated practices and symbolic actions, so also ecclesial liturgies shape us through sacred rhythms, directing our affections toward the Kingdom of God. If doctrine is to form disciples, it must take flesh in rituals and rhythms that direct the heart, body, and vision toward Christ, shaping a people whose loves are rightly ordered by the Spirit.

Faithful doctrine helps cultivate a holy habitus, a way of being attuned to God's presence in the world. In doing so, it reinforces the chapter's central claim that doctrine functions as spiritual pedagogy, shaping not only belief, but the whole person for life in God's future. Formation happens through the body and imagination as much as the mind. Doctrine reorders desire not merely for individuals, but within the shared life of the Church that spiritual formation is deeply entangled with the reordering of desire, a process not only personal but profoundly communal. This transformation of desire occurs within the life of the Church, where prayer, doctrine, and shared vulnerability reorient the affections of the whole community toward divine love. Contemplative prayer becomes the crucible in which disordered loves are purified and drawn into divine longing. This is not a denial of desire, but its transfiguration, a process of spiritual pedagogy whereby desire is not erased but refined through shared prayer and participation in God's life. Doctrine, then, is not simply about mastering content but rather about reordering desire to Trinitarian participation, where the believer is drawn into the relational life of God, reinforcing the chapter's theme of divine love and communion. Participation is about being mastered, and reshaped, by the love of God in Christ through the Spirit, whose work aligns our desires with God's own.

Doctrine and the Senses: Theological Foundations

This embodied remembering draws us into theological ground that insists doctrine must engage the whole person, body, mind, and imagination. If doctrine forms us for God's future, it must mirror the logic of the Incarnation: it must take shape through the body, in community, and across time. The Church's faith is not merely stated in words; it is sung, tasted, prayed, touched, and inhabited. Doctrine lives through sacramental grace and sensory participation. It is learned not only in seminar rooms but in the fragrant oil of healing, the pressure of kneeling, the texture of bread, and the icon's quiet gaze.

Just as the Word became flesh, so must doctrine. Doctrine must take shape in the liturgies, ethics, and embodied witness of the Church, becoming visible in acts of mercy, audible in the cries for justice, and tangible in the sacramental life of the Body of Christ. As the Word did not remain distant or disembodied, so doctrine must enter the world of human experience, language, and flesh, formed in community and practiced in love. It is only when doctrine is enfleshed in the rhythms of the Church's daily life that it truly reflects the incarnational logic it proclaims. God speaks not in abstraction but in embodied presence, as Athanasius and Irenaeus both insist in their incarnational theologies, not in theological propositions but in person. The Incarnate Christ is the visible image of the invisible God, the living doctrine of divine love enfleshed in history. If Christ is the Word made flesh, then faithful doctrine must become the language of love made visible, palpable, and audible in the Church's life. Doctrine is not frozen thought in time but a rhythm of participation that is everlasting, a grammar of grace rehearsed in the postures of prayer and the music of the liturgy.

This sacramental logic finds deep resonance in the theological tradition. The Trinity is not an abstract puzzle, but a relational and economic reality that must be encountered through the embodied life of the Church. The economic Trinity, God's actions in history, grounds doctrine in practices like the Eucharist, communal worship, and gestures of hospitality. These sensory and sacramental acts are not mere symbols but are themselves formative: they make the divine life visible, audible, and touchable. In this light, doctrine becomes not merely a statement about God but a choreography of participation in God's self-giving life. An emphasis on the economic Trinity underlines that God's self-giving love is not merely doctrinal in content but sacramental in presence, integrated into the Church's embodied worship and formative of believers through tangible, sensory practices, inviting the Church to reflect this divine relationality in her sensory, embodied practices of worship and formation. This is the shape of God's love shared with creation. Doctrine, therefore, must reflect the relational and economic movement of God's self-giving. The economic Trinity is the immanent Trinity grounds doctrine in divine action. What God does in history, healing, sending, pouring out the Spirit, is who God is eternally: a communion of love. Doctrine becomes not just reflection but participation in divine encounter, as it engages the Church in the relational and economic movement of God's self-giving love, made tangible through sacramental presence and communal formation.

Sarah Coakley draws this into the life of prayer, offering a deeply integrated vision where spiritual formation and theological understanding converge. In her theology of contemplation, she offers a vision where doctrine is intensified through silence, not bypassed. In the stillness of bodily surrender, the believer is caught up in the Spirit's movement of self-giving love. Here, doctrine takes root not in propositions alone, but in desire transformed, in the gradual reordering of the heart through attention to divine presence. Doctrine forms through *théologie totale*: a theology that includes gender, body, and desire in its scope. The Spirit does not bypass the body; the Spirit sanctifies it, drawing even our desires into divine resonance.

Doctrine forms, not by mastering content but by cultivating attentiveness, surrender, and receptivity to divine beauty. Doctrine is a pedagogy of the body and imagination, shaping a Church that gazes, waits, and desires God rightly, who sees in iconography a contemplative pedagogy, one that resonates a vision of desire and embodiment.

Thus, doctrine forms not by mastering content but by cultivating attentiveness, surrender, and receptivity to divine beauty. Doctrine is a pedagogy of the body and imagination, shaping a Church that gazes, waits, and desires God rightly. The icon is not a decoration but a door: it teaches us to see, not by grasping but by attending. Doctrine, like the icon, forms a kind of vision, training our gaze to perceive divine mystery, not as object but as gift. Prayer before the icon teaches the Church to be mastered by God's beauty, allowing that beauty to form not only her aesthetic sense but also her theological understanding. By training the gaze toward divine mystery, icons shape the Church's capacity to perceive and receive doctrine as a lived, relational, and grace-filled reality rather than to master God with definitions and concepts. After all, "A God comprehended is no God at all," says Francis Turretin.

Doctrine rightly formed shapes communities toward reconciliation, joy, and justice. Belief that remains disembodied cannot transform the world. When doctrine takes flesh in action, it becomes what it was always meant to be: a shared habitus of love, rooted in divine generosity and directed toward the neighbor.

This transformative vision has ancient roots. Gregory of Nyssa describes doctrine as ascent, an image that powerfully reinforces the chapter's vision of doctrine as an ongoing, dynamic process of formation. Theological understanding is not a final possession but a continual stretching toward divine mystery, aligning with this chapter's claim that doctrine is a pedagogy of transformation rather than a static system of belief: not possession of static truth but the soul's stretching toward the infinite beauty of God. Theological understanding is not a final arrival but an ever-deepening participation in divine mystery. Similarly, Augustine, in his *Confessions*, presents doctrine as prayerful memory, truth that does not inflate the mind but reorders the heart. For Augustine, doctrine becomes wisdom when it directs all of life toward the God who is love.

All these voices converge in a vision of doctrine that is not disembodied but doxological, not detached but sacramental. At Pentecost, the Church was not given a manual or blueprint in the form of a creed. She was given a flame, a sound, a rushing breath. The senses were ignited. The Spirit descended not as a text but as event and encounter. From that moment, the Church's doctrine has been forged not merely in intellectual clarity, but in sensory transformation: a body learning to hear the Word in many tongues, to see the invisible in bread and wine, to feel the divine touch in the oil of anointing.

Doctrine, then, is the grammar of participation, a grammar progressively revealed. Whether through the icon's gaze, the stillness of prayer, the Eucharistic table, or the longing ascent toward divine mystery, this participatory grammar takes shape in the Church's life as a choreography of grace and transformation. It shapes not just what the Church thinks, but how she loves and what she longs for. It orders our senses not by restriction but by resonance, tuning our eyes to beauty, our ears to mercy, our bodies to grace. Doctrine made flesh becomes not only the Church's confession, but her formation: a reality progressively unveiled through the Incarnational, iconographic, and communal practices explored in this section, each theological voice contributing to a grammar of divine love that is embodied, sacramental, and pedagogical, a way of being in the world that reflects, enacts, and anticipates God's future.

Connexionalism and the Practice of Friendship

Flowing from a sensory and sacramental vision of doctrine, we arrive at its communal consequence: doctrine as the social fabric of divine friendship. Doctrine is not a solitary insight but a shared inheritance, shaping a people into a living communion. It forms not only the thoughts of individuals but the affections, practices, and relationships that constitute the Body of Christ. Doctrine is relational grammar, the speech of a Church that is learning to love. This grammar will unfold more fully across the theological voices that follow, each contributing to a pedagogical vision of doctrine as embodied, communal, and spiritually formative in the shape of the Triune God.

From its inception, the Church's doctrinal life was forged in shared meals, remembered stories, mutual forgiveness, and the Spirit's gifts dispersed among all. In the Wesleyan tradition, this ecclesial vision takes the form of connexionalism, a network of holy friendships bound by shared doctrine, mutual encouragement, and mission. Connexionalism is not a fixed hierarchical structure of episcopacy but a living contrast to it, eschewing rigid, top-down authority in favor of a Spirit-formed network of reciprocal relationships. It points to a form of ecclesial life where authority emerges through shared discernment, vulnerability, and mutual accountability, embodying doctrine as a formative and pedagogical structure that shapes the Church's communal life. Rather than consolidating power in office, connexionalism distributes it through covenantal bonds of love and mission, witnessing to the counter-cultural nature of the Triune God's communion.

Unlike rigid top-down systems of ecclesial governance and control that can obscure the relational nature of the Church, Wesley's connexionalism points to a counter-cultural vision of ecclesial life marked by horizontal bonds of vulnerable trust, shared discernment, and collaborative mission. It resists institutionalism by embodying the Triune rhythm of giving and receiving, of mutual indwelling and shared joy. In this way, doctrine becomes not only instruction but infrastructure, a relational architecture that embodies the grammar of divine friendship introduced at the start of this section. This spiritual framework forms a community that doesn't merely articulate beliefs but lives them out in mutual accountability, trust, and love. Through friendship, doctrine builds the Church not just in thought but in the lived structures of grace that reflect the Triune communion. The Church, in this vision, is a web of grace, an interlacing of spiritual friendships that reflect the perichoretic life of the Trinity itself.

For John Wesley, Christian friendship was not peripheral; it was a means of grace, a connexion where doctrine became embodied in daily life. Friendship was perhaps the truest sacramental signifier, a visible means by which we embody the truth that we have been made as "transcripts of the Trinity" (Wesley). This is a metaphor suggesting that the Church is called not merely to speak about God but to visibly reflect and participate in the relational, communal friendship that marks the life of the Triune God. Just as a transcript conveys the content of an original in another form, so the Church, through the practices of friendship, mirrors the perichoretic love of the Triune God.

This motif of friendship has both pedagogical and ecclesiological weight: friendship becomes the contagious means by which doctrine is not only learned but joyously lived, forming a Church whose very structure bears witness to divine communion in the perfect love of God. In class meetings, love feasts, and shared prayer, doctrine was not taught as theory but lived as relational and vulnerable trust and discipline. Wesley understood that Christian formation happened through Spirit-animated communities of care and correction, joy and suffering. Faithful doctrine, as the grammar of love, was not imposed from above but given and circulated through friendship, shaping character through shared vulnerability and hospitality.

Wesley's theological instinct aligns with the deep Trinitarian current of the Church, reinforcing this chapter's central vision of doctrine as relational, embodied, and formative within the communal life of God. The Trinity is not a remote brainteaser to solve, but the structure of salvation itself, God's life poured out into communion and fellowship. Theological doctrine, then, is not speculation about divine categories, but the formation of people into divine friendship. The Church is a community of relational participation in God's life, and friendship is one of its primary sacraments.

Friendship is the soul's ascent into divine intimacy. True friendship draws the person beyond self-enclosure, stretching the heart toward participation in God's inexhaustible love. Doctrine, in this key, becomes the choreography of that ascent, the script by which souls are taught to move in harmony with divine desire.

Similarly, Augustine's *De Trinitate* suggests that human relationships mirror the inner life of God. Friendship is theological because it reflects the eternal giving and receiving of the Trinity. For Augustine, the Church is called not only to confess the Trinity but to embody it, to become a communion where persons, in love, reflect the divine life in mutual delight and gift.

Yet this mutuality must be guarded against distortion. Hierarchical projections of God deform the Church's life. The Trinity is not a monarchy to be copied but a mutual indwelling of perichoretic love, and the Church must mirror this not with domination but with Spirit-shaped communion and hospitality. Ecclesial friendship is the antidote to authoritarian ecclesiology, it is the rehearsal of freedom in love that marks the New Creation.

Doctrine should not serve as a tool of exclusion but should form communities of reciprocity, where every voice and gift are honored. Friendship, in this light, is not just affection, it is ecclesial architecture of communion, embodying the relational grammar of doctrine introduced at the outset of this section. It gives tangible shape to the Church's theological convictions, turning love into structure and communion into witness. Friendship that reflects the life of the Trinity is a structural expression of doctrine's formative power to build up the Body of Christ through mutuality, vulnerability, and shared mission. It builds the space in which truth is spoken in love, embodying the section's initial vision of doctrine as a relational architecture, an ecclesial grammar shaped by the Spirit's choreography of holy friendship, where wounds are healed, and joy becomes communal.

This is why doctrine, at its core, is about forming affections as much as forging a grammar of faith. It teaches the Church how to dwell in the oikodome, the household, of Triune love: a community marked by shared meals, mutual discernment, Spirit-led forgiveness, and reconciling joy. Doctrine is not abstract content to be downloaded; it is the language of a people becoming holy together. Through friendship, doctrine takes flesh, revealing that the life of God is not hoarded in heaven but diffused in the hearts of those who break bread, bear burdens, and bless one another in love.

The Church's shared life, its friendships, its conflicts, its reconciliations, is not a mere echo of the Triune life, but a participation in God's very being. The friendships formed by doctrine are not incidental. They are sacramental signs of God's self-communication, embodied expressions of doctrine made flesh.

Liturgical-Historical Bridge: Ancient Sources of Sensory Faith

The embodied and relational life of doctrine, manifest in holy friendships and Spirit-shaped communities, does not arise in isolation. It is the flowering of deep roots: the Church's long memory of faith enacted, not only believed. From the beginning, Christian doctrine has been transmitted not simply in creedal form but through embodied worship, sensory practices, and communal participation. These embodied practices are not peripheral; they are primary modes of doctrinal formation, enacting the choreography of grace by which the Church learns to move in rhythm with divine love, shaping the imagination, affections, and habits of the faithful. In the gestures of worship, the rhythms of liturgy, and the beauty of sacred art and music, the Church does not merely express doctrine, it learns, inhabits, and is formed by it. The ancient Church offers not just precedent but theological grounding: for example, Irenaeus of Lyons who wrote that "our teaching is in accord with the Eucharist, and the Eucharist confirms our teaching," grounding doctrine in embodied worship: doctrine is not an idea to be grasped, but a life to be inhabited. The Fathers understood what the Church today must recover: that the worship of God is doctrine's native soil.

From the earliest generations, salvation was never imagined as escape from the material world, but as its transfiguration. Ignatius of Antioch, on his way to martyrdom, confessed in his *Letter to the Smyrnaeans* (6-8), that the Eucharist was the glue of the Church's unity, the place where Christ's Body, broken and given, gathered the faithful into one cruciform communion. For Ignatius, the ecclesial body did not merely receive the risen Christ; it became his Body through the sacrament, manifesting the mystery of doctrine in the liturgy of life.

Justin Martyr, in his *First Apology*, describes Christian worship as a profoundly embodied event: Scriptures proclaimed aloud, prayers raised, bread and wine brought forward, blessed, and consumed. This was not spectacle or private devotion, but participation in the Logos, a rational, sacramental liturgy where the truth of doctrine was not dissected but encountered. For Justin, doctrine was not recited apart from worship; it was disclosed through it.

The Cappadocian Fathers, especially Gregory of Nyssa, developed this further. Gregory saw creation itself as sacramental, a mystical vision that affirms this chapter's claim that doctrine takes embodied, sensory form. Creation is not neutral matter but a divine medium through which the soul is drawn into ever-deepening participation in God's mystery, a vision that sees doctrine not as detached truth but as a transformative, an incarnational journey in a world charged with divine presence, drawing the soul beyond itself toward God. Christian life can be understood as an unending ascent into mystery, where the body and its practices are not barriers but instruments of transfiguration. The Spirit does not discard matter; the Spirit illuminates it, sanctifying the material as the very means through which God forms and communicates divine life. This affirmation supports the chapter's larger claim that doctrine is not abstract or cerebral, but incarnational and participatory, shaped in the tangible, embodied experiences of worship, sacrament, and ecclesial communion. Doctrine, in this mystical vision, is not abstract system but the ordering of desire toward divine beauty, a journey of participation, not possession or control.

These patristic voices resonate deeply with the Wesleyan imagination. John Wesley did not forge a new theological path so much as he revived and reclaimed the ancient one; as he writes in his sermon "The Character of a Methodist," his aim was to revive the essence of primitive

Christianity, grounded in the practices and spirit of the early Church; he walked faithfully in the footsteps of "Primitive Christianity," reinvigorating its sacramental instincts with the fire of God's love. Like the Fathers, Wesley believed that grace is mediated through the tangible, that faithful doctrine is learned not by memorization but by prayer, song, meal, and touch. His theology of the means of grace was a reanimation of the Church's ancient conviction: that the Spirit sanctifies not only the soul but the senses.

Wesley's liturgical sensibility echoes Augustine's vision, further illustrating how doctrinal understanding is formed not through abstract speculation, but through worship that shapes the affections and reorders desire in *Confessions*, where knowledge of God arises from a heart tuned in worship to sing God's praise. Augustine teaches that true understanding begins not in speculation but in humility and praise. For both Augustine and Wesley, friendship with God and neighbor is not a byproduct of doctrine but its goal. And that friendship is nurtured in the liturgical rhythms of the Church, where hearts are warmed, bodies are lifted, and minds are renewed.

In this light, Wesleyan theology appears not as a kind of theological innovation that creates out of nothing, but as faithful inheritance. The Church's doctrine takes flesh in the sanctified body, where memory becomes motion and belief (faith) becomes song. From the early martyrs and mystics to the hymns and class meetings of Methodism, doctrine as the grammar of faith filled with God's love has always been embedded in the Church's sensory life. This enduring pattern underscores the continuity between patristic and Wesleyan theology, not as divergent traditions, but as a shared stream of incarnational formation. Wesley's retrieval of ancient practices reflects not innovation but recovery, a faithful reenactment of the Church's earliest understanding that doctrine is not abstract theory but embodied participation. What the Fathers practiced in incense and icon, what Wesley recovered in Eucharist and friendship, the Spirit still breathes into the Body of Christ today.

Doctrine is not content to be thought; it longs to be sung, prayed in the silence of the heart, anointed through gestures of healing, and shared at the Eucharistic table, a participatory grammar of divine love that finds its fullest expression in the Spirit's pedagogy of worship, embodiment, and communion. In this communion of ancient and future praise, the Church remembers forward, carrying her doctrine in hands lifted in worship, in hearts broken open in love, and in bodies joined to the living Christ.

Icons, Music, Liturgy: The Spirit's Sensory Gifts

Doctrine, when it comes fully alive, becomes visible in icon, audible in music, and kinesthetic in liturgy, each a sensory expression of the Spirit's formative work in the Church. These modes are not merely aesthetic; they are pedagogical, shaping the faithful through embodied participation in divine truth. These practices are not embellishments to theology; they are its embodiment, central to the Church's transmission of doctrine through lived, sensory encounter, the Spirit's own sensory grammar of divine love. In them, theology is not merely taught but encountered, performed, and sung. These are not illustrations of doctrine; they are its form of transmission, shaping not only thought but imagination, memory, and longing.

Icons: Seeing the Word Made Visible

Theology is painted in the stillness of an icon. Icons do with color and light what Scripture does with language and story: they embody the Church's participatory grammar, shaping theological imagination through visual encounter just as Scripture shapes it through narrative. Icons teach not simply by representing but by inviting the beholder into contemplation, becoming pedagogical windows through which doctrine is not only seen but internalized. Icons render visible the mystery of the Word made flesh. In beholding an icon, the Church does not merely observe, it attends. The icon does not depict absence; it reveals presence. It trains the eye to perceive transfigured reality: the world suffused with divine light. Here, the act of seeing becomes contemplation, and the image becomes a window into the Kingdom.

In this visual theology, we find echoes of Gregory of Nyssa's mysticism of the gaze, where contemplation is not stasis but movement. Icons are not merely historical or aesthetic artifacts; they are portals through which the Spirit lifts the soul toward union with Christ. In this contemplative act of seeing, the icon shapes theological perception, inviting the beholder to attend, receive, and be formed by divine beauty, which itself becomes a pedagogy of doctrine.

Music: Doctrine Sung into the Soul

If icons are theology painted, then music is theology breathed. Sacred music is not the background of Christian life; it is its pulse. From the ancient cadences of Gregorian chant to the poetic power of Wesleyan hymnody, the Church has always known that doctrine sung becomes doctrine remembered, and doctrine desired. Music shapes the affections by embedding theological truths in rhythm and tone, reaching the heart through repetition and emotional resonance, showing that when doctrine is sung, it takes root in memory and awakens desire, as explored earlier in the chapter. In this way, song becomes both catechesis and longing, doctrine not only understood but loved.

Augustine, in *Confessions* (Book X) and *De Musica* (Book VI) affirms that music not only delights but elevates the soul. Singing, he writes, is a form of prayer intensified, for "he who sings prays twice." Melody and meter shape the memory, forming not only the intellect but the affections. When the Church sings the faith, she aligns heart and voice with the music of heaven. Hymns such as Charles Wesley's "Love Divine, All Loves Excelling" are not ornamentation, they are theological formation in lyrical form.

Music also embodies the Spirit's breath. In song, the community inhales from the Spirit the truth that is the energy of God's love and exhales from the Spirit's breath endless praise to the Triune God. The Church learns to desire rightly by singing the beauty of holiness. Doctrine, when chanted or harmonized, does not become less serious, it becomes more deeply enfleshed, reaching the imagination through tone and cadence, rhythm and refrain.

Liturgy: Doctrine in Motion

Liturgy is theology enacted, an embodied synthesis of icon and music, integrating the visual and auditory dimensions of doctrine into the Church's bodily rhythm of grace, and embodied pedagogy through which doctrine is not only spoken but lived, integrating and expanding the theological formation initiated by icon and music. While icons shape the eye to see divine beauty and music trains the ears so that the heart desires truth, liturgy gathers these senses into a sacred rhythm of movement and word, teaching the whole body to dwell in the love of God. Liturgy is shaping the Church's spiritual imagination and habits of love.

Liturgy is the Church's choreography of grace, where the body learns doctrine through gesture, posture, silence, and sacrament. In kneeling to confess, in standing to proclaim, in crossing the forehead with holy oil or receiving the Eucharist with open hands, the Church performs her theology, not abstractly but bodily. Liturgy is not merely symbolic action; it is the Spirit's school of formation.

Liturgy is the space where Trinitarian doctrine becomes relational reality. The liturgy not only proclaims the Trinity, it re-forms the people of God into its image. It is the rhythm by which we are drawn into the eternal circulation of divine love, enacted through Word and table, intercession and thanksgiving. The shape of the liturgy becomes the shape of doctrine lived. Liturgy is structured encounter with God.

Here, Wesleyan and patristic sensibilities converge again. John Wesley's liturgical theology, shaped by ancient Christian practice, was animated by this very conviction: that grace is not only received in thought, but in movement and song, in water and wine, in the regular rhythms of communal worship. For Wesley, to kneel at the rail, to sing with the congregation, to share in the prayers of the people, these were all forms of doctrinal formation.

A Sensory Pedagogy of Love

Icons, music, and liturgy form the sensory heart of Christian pedagogy, through seeing, hearing, and enacting, they shape how doctrine is perceived, remembered, and embodied in practices through which doctrine becomes flesh, shaping the Church for communion with God and formation in God's future. Doctrine is carried not as data but as delight. They inscribe theology on the body, stir it in the heart, and echo it in the imagination. Doctrine is not only what the Church affirms; it is what the Church sees, sings, and enacts, a language of faith shaped in the respiration of the Spirit and the gestures of worship.

These practices are not marginal. They are sacramental means of doctrinal formation, through them, the Spirit forms the Church into a living sign of God's future, shaping the Body of Christ to bear witness to the coming Kingdom in embodied, communal ways, where the Spirit teaches through beauty, movement, and sound. Doctrine lives when it is painted in gold, carried on melody, and traced in the sign of the cross. In these gifts, the Spirit not only instructs the mind but awakens the soul to the joy of knowing God.

The Church as Icon of the Trinity

All of this, icon, music, liturgy, friendship, memory, leads us to the Church's deepest vocation: to become a living icon of Triune love. This section gathers the chapter's sensory and sacramental threads into an ecclesiological synthesis, portraying the Church not merely as recipient of doctrine but as its visible expression, a Spirit-formed body through whom the grammar of divine love is lived, enacted, and made flesh in the world. The Church does not merely speak doctrine; she embodies it. Having traced the embodied forms of doctrinal formation, we now turn to the ecclesiological heart of these practices: the Church herself as the Spirit-formed community in whom doctrine becomes visible, audible, and relational. These sensory and sacramental practices are not ends in themselves. They converge to form the Church as a living pedagogy, a community where doctrine takes on flesh, training hearts and bodies to dwell in the rhythm of divine love. They are formative pathways, drawing the Church into communion with the God she proclaims.

To confess the Trinity is to confess that the very being of God is communion, Father, Son, and Holy Spirit, eternally indwelling one another in infinite, vulnerable love. This divine life is not static essence but dynamic exchange: the joyous perichoresis of self-giving and receiving. Doctrine gives faithful language to this truth, but the Church enacts it. The Church becomes an icon of the Trinity when she lives this rhythm, forgiving, serving, celebrating, reconciling, and offering herself for the world.

The Church lives only as she shares in the life of the Triune God. Communion is not optional, it is her ontology. After all, the very being of God is love. In gathering, at the Spirit's prompting, the Church becomes a sacrament of divine relationality, enfleshing Trinitarian love in history. What God does in salvation history reveals who God is eternally. If this is true, then every moment of communion, every act of reconciliation, Eucharistic sharing, and Spirit-formed friendship, is a participation in God's own life. Ecclesiology, then, is not a separate branch of theology, it is doctrine in motion, doctrine as Spirit-choreographed life.

Catherine LaCugna describes the Church as the "living icon of God's self-giving." Thus, orthodoxy and orthopraxy are inseparable: we know the Trinity not through abstract speculation but by becoming a people whose life mirrors divine communion. The Church is icon only to the extent that she lives as sacrament of God's love, vulnerable, hospitable, relational, and joyful. Right doctrine is not reduced to conceptual accuracy; it is relational fidelity. The Church is not merely the audience of God's revelation but a stage upon which the drama of redemption unfolds. She participates in the divine drama of love, where doctrine unfolds not as monologue but as communal embodiment, a script embodied in worship, mission, and mutuality. The Church does not only say true things about God; she acts them out, becoming a visible sign of the Triune story.

This performance is not institutional choreography but mystical transformation. True knowledge of God comes not through analytical precision but through the gradual transfiguration of the soul in love, a mystical ascent into divine beauty that mirrors this chapter's claim that doctrine is a dynamic and participatory process. The Church becomes the community being transformed together, ascending, through doctrine as participation, into the very life of God where love shapes and sustains all formation, as it were, into the life of God. Her unity is not primarily structural but sacramental, a sign of her ongoing participation in the unitive life of Father, Son, and Spirit.

This unity does not erase diversity but celebrates it, echoing the Trinitarian vision of unity-in-difference where distinct persons dwell in perfect communion. Such theological vision forms the Church to witness not through uniformity but through relational fidelity, doctrine embodied in the harmony of difference that reflects the mutuality of Father, Son, and Spirit. The Church, then, is not made one in unitive love through institutional conformity but through the contagious gift of fellowship, a communion that reflects the mutual love and distinction of the divine persons. Doctrine, in this sense, is not a closed system but a dynamic choreography, the rhythm by which the Church learns to love as God loves.

Wesleyan holiness is precisely this: love perfected in communion, doctrine formed in the Spirit-shaped grammar of love made flesh in the Church's worship, friendships, and justice-bearing witness. For Wesley, sanctification is not private piety but shared joy, a holiness that joins the believer to God, neighbor, and creation in love. The sanctified Church does not merely reflect the Trinity; she participates in it. In her prayers and friendships, in her sacraments and songs, in her justice and her mercy, the Church becomes, in her flesh and frailty, a breathing icon of the eternal dance, radiant with the life of God for the life of the world.

Apocalyptic Unveiling: Groaning Toward Glory

Having beheld the Church as a living icon of Triune love, we must now follow that icon into the world's sorrow. This marks a shift from ecclesiology to eschatology, where doctrine moves from contemplative formation within the Body to public witness amid the fractures of history. The icon now steps into lament, carrying hope into the world's groaning. The Church does not reflect God's life only in stained glass and sacred song; she also bears witness in tears, ashes, and protest. To be icon is also to be witness, to live faithfully in a groaning creation, bearing the wounds of history even as she proclaims the "hope of glory."

The icon of the Church is painted not only in gold but also in grief. Doctrine, if it is true, must learn to groan, a grammar of hope shaped in suffering, tuned to lament and longing, and speaking the dialect of Spirit-breathed resilience grammar of hope formed in suffering, extending the participatory grammar explored earlier in this chapter. Here, that grammar is shaped not only by beauty and praise but by lament, protest, and Spirit-breathed resilience, to speak the dialect of lament, longing, and resilient hope. It must echo the cry of creation itself, which, as Paul writes, is groaning in labor pains, awaiting redemption. The Spirit, too, groans with sighs too deep for words. In such a world, doctrine cannot be detached speculation; it must become poetic courage, naming both the radiance and the rupture, both the already and the not-yet.

In his signature work, *The Prophetic Imagination*, Walter Brueggemann reminds us that prophetic imagination is rooted in lament, poetry, and hope. Theology is not passive reflection but imaginative resistance and generative formation as imaginative, disruptive, and hope-generating speech, which re-perceives reality and calls forth newness, informs a broader vision of doctrine not merely as critique but as creative eschatological formation that is not about forecasting future events but about re-perceiving reality. It dares to see what empire hides, to speak what empire silences. Prophetic vision generates hope by disrupting numbness and dismantling false inevitabilities. It calls

- 94 -

forth newness in the ruins. When the Church embraces this vocation, doctrine becomes prophetic speech, no longer a defensive system of the past but a new song in a weary land, a language born in lament and sustained by stubborn joy.

In this prophetic mode, Karl Rahner insists that theology must be both mystical and historical. It cannot remain in the clouds; it must arise from the dust, from prayer rooted in wounds, and from vision forged in the cross of history. Doctrine becomes faithful when it bears history's weight and walks with the crucified, refusing both denial and despair. The prophets of Israel, whom Rahner echoes, did not speak from neutral ground. Like an icon shaped by the light of God's future, the prophets saw not only what was, but what could be, naming reality from within the grammar of love and the hope of divine becoming. They saw from the future, their tongues ignited with divine fire, breaking open complacency and calling a people to awaken.

Doctrine becomes apocalyptic when it unveils what is hidden, when, like the icon, it discloses divine truth not through abstraction but through participation, suffering, and hope. Just as the icon reveals presence through form and light, apocalyptic doctrine unveils glory beneath grief and promise beneath ruin, another mode of theological vision by which the Church learns to see God's future breaking into the now. As doctrine becomes apocalyptic it reveals the glory stirring beneath ruin, the Spirit breathing beneath silence, the God who comes even now.

This is not a doctrine of escapism but of perpetual becoming. Eschatology reminds us that the soul's journey into God is never finished, a vision that underscores this chapter's claim that doctrine is always becoming into God and is never complete until all are gathered into divine love. His theology of ongoing transformation calls the Church to remain open to surprise, ever attuned to the Spirit's renewing grace, ever stretching toward the fullness of glory.

Miroslav Volf calls this posture "embracing memory," a way of holding suffering without vengeance, of remembering in a way that opens to reconciliation and justice. Doctrine must not be weaponized to preserve the status quo.

It must become ferment for renewal, a vision of hope fermenting in the fissures of injustice, pressing toward the Kingdom where all are restored.

Such doctrine evolves, not because truth that God is love changes, but because the Spirit's dynamic work continually renews the Church's language and life. The Spirit holds fast to the heart of the Gospel, preserving its essence while continually renewing its voice for each generation even as she reshapes its form for each generation, preserving its essence while igniting new expressions of grace and witness. As God's love is unchangeably faithful, the Spirit who keeps pouring the energy of God's love over all creation is not static. She is not the curator of museum relics but the flame who transfigures dead words into living witness. She breathes through the cracks in our formulations, in the silence before an icon, in the swell of a hymn, in the embrace of friendship, in the touch of healing oil, re-igniting tired truths with fresh fire. The Spirit reveals again and again what Christ has already made known: that love will not fail, and that justice is still possible because the end of God's justice is always love.

In every act of Eucharistic defiance, each a form of doctrine made flesh, in every protest march that sings lament and refuses despair, in every moment when hope is risked again, doctrine is made new. Not discarded but transfigured. In the hands of the Spirit, the Church learns to see anew, to speak again, to groan toward glory, trusting that even now, even here, the Kingdom is nearby.

Eucharist as Apocalyptic Memory and Future

The Eucharist is where doctrine is digested, where the participatory, sensory pedagogy of the Spirit reaches its most intimate form. In this act of shared nourishment, doctrine is not merely heard or seen, but taken into the body, becoming the living grammar of grace. Here, time bends and eternity draws near: past sacrifice meets future glory, and the risen Christ is not merely remembered as event but received as food, the feast of new and unending life. In bread broken and wine poured, the Church does not simply recite beliefs.

She eats them. She takes into herself the One who is truth, communion, and life.

In this holy meal, doctrine becomes presence, not a concept to be parsed, but a reality to be encountered. It is not abstract but embodied: enacted, received, and shared. Echoing the chapter's vision of doctrine as performance, this presence becomes a tactile witness to divine love, passed between trembling hands and lived in the communion of saints. The Church receives not a symbol but the living Christ, who gives himself again and again, not to be dissected, but to be tasted, digested, and shared. As Henri de Lubac famously said, "The eucharist makes the church." In this act, doctrine is not argued but ingested. Christ is not only proclaimed but consumed. The Body of Christ becomes what it eats: communion for a fragmented world.

In the Eucharist, memory is not mere mental recall but sacramental transformation. The Church is not only remembering Christ; she is re-membered into Christ, drawn together across time, space, and difference into the one Body shaped by love. This Eucharistic transformation is not simply personal but ecclesial, even cosmic. The Church's identity is fundamentally Eucharistic: at the Table, the Spirit gathers believers into the Body across time and space, making visible the Kingdom's eruption into history. The Table, then, is no mere symbol, it is an apocalyptic unveiling echoing the vision of revelation and groaning hope. As apocalyptic doctrine unveils divine truth through suffering and promise, so too does the Eucharist, revealing the inbreaking of God's future in the form of broken bread and poured wine reveal the inbreaking of God's future through broken bread and poured wine. Here, the Church does not merely remember, she beholds the unveiled mystery of Christ's love made flesh for the world. The Eucharist is the eschatological heart of doctrine made flesh. It is an apocalypse, an unveiling of what is already true and yet still coming.

The Church can, as Hans Urs von Balthasar suggested, be envisaged as a "theo-dramatic act," and the Eucharist as its climactic scene, where doctrine becomes performance, theology becomes drama, and love becomes edible, a vivid sign of doctrine's sensory pedagogy and embodied theology. In the liturgical drama of Word and Table, the Church not only speaks of God; she participates in the divine performance of grace. The Eucharist is the stage where the Triune life is enacted in gestures of offering, receiving, and sending. In Word and Table, theology becomes liturgy, love becomes edible. Within this relational vision, we experience the Eucharist as the ultimate expression of Trinitarian life shared with the world. It is where theology becomes praise and where divine mystery becomes self-giving presence. The Eucharist, in her vision, is the place where the Church is most truly herself: a communion grounded in the overflowing love of God.

And if the Eucharist gathers us into God's life, it also stretches us toward God's future. Karl Rahner calls the Eucharist the "real symbol" of God's future, not a placeholder but a sacramental actualization of grace. In this meal, the Church tastes not only forgiveness but the transfigured future: the world to come breaking into the present, the eschaton offered in a cup. Doctrine here is no longer theory; it is edible eschatology, a sacramental act that remembers Christ's past and anticipates his promised future, uniting the Church in the hope of glory as a foretaste of the world made new. The Table is not the conclusion of faith but its beginning, the sustenance of a people living together in the promised hope of New Creation.

The Eucharist is not a static ritual but a dynamic ascent. It is the nourishment of the soul on its journey into God's inexhaustible beauty. The bread and wine are not the conclusion but the beginning, the food of pilgrimage toward the divine embrace. The Eucharist provides the grammar of belief, a Spirit-shaped pedagogy where doctrine becomes formation in communion, where doctrine becomes embodied, enacted, and eschatologically charged. The Eucharist does not only make the Church; it forms her grammar of belief. Here, the Spirit gathers memory, body, and hope into one holy communion. Doctrine becomes the stuff of sacrament: ingested truth, broken grace, embodied hope. At the Table, the Church is reformed again into the icon of the world to come.

To confess doctrine, then, is not merely to articulate truth but to inhabit it, formed by the Eucharistic table and shaped by grace into a lived confession that embodies what has been received at the Eucharistic table, where doctrine becomes the culminating expression of the Spirit-formed, sacramentally enacted pedagogy that shapes the Church for God's future. To confess is to live into the truth, formed by grace and nourished in communion, where belief is not only proclaimed but performed. It is the Spirit's choreography of holy life, performed in friendships, sacraments, music, liturgies, and witness. It is a grammar of communion that teaches the Body to see, to serve, and to sing the world into transfigured possibility.

Formed by memory, corrected in love, enacted through the senses, and fulfilled in Eucharistic hope, doctrine becomes the living confession of a Church on pilgrimage. It is the song of the saints and the schooling of the soul. From painted icon to whispered hymn, from shared bread to shared tears, the Church lives doctrine not by abstraction but by incarnation, becoming what she professes.

When doctrine breathes, it forms disciples who are iconographers of grace, artisans of hope, and participants in the Triune Love of God from everlasting to everlasting.

Conclusion: Doctrine as the Spirit's Choreography of Love

Having just traced the Eucharist as the culminating site of doctrine made flesh, we now reaffirm: doctrine, at its deepest, is not a system to be memorized but a life to be lived, a grammar of grace nourished by sacrament and shaped by praise that forms a people into the likeness of Christ. In this chapter, we have traced the formational power of doctrine, not as abstract theory but as a Spirit-shaped pedagogy that trains the Church in faith, hope, and love. Doctrine begins in memory and unfolds in embodied witness; it sings through sacred music, shines in icons, moves in liturgy, and finds its fullness at the Eucharistic table.

Through this journey, we have seen that doctrine is not a static set of truths. It is dynamic participation in the self-giving life of the Triune God. The Church becomes the icon of this divine life, not by perfect clarity of statement, but by faithful formation, by learning to forgive, to welcome, to sing, to serve, and to suffer together in hope. Doctrine takes flesh as it forms friendships, stirs desire, and prepares the Church to become a holy offering for the world.

We have also affirmed that doctrine must groan with creation, must lament, protest, and hope within the fractures of history. True doctrine is prophetic and apocalyptic, not a departure from the Church's grammar, but its Spirit-breathed unfolding across time. It is faithful to the core of God's self-revealing love, yet always speaking anew into the crises, laments, and longings of history. Faithful doctrine is not only responsive to history's wounds but unveils God's redemptive future through imaginative witness and hope, it unveils hidden grace; resists despair and opens a future not of our making but of God's promise. It dares to speak light into shadow and invites the Church to embody the coming Kingdom even now.

And at the Eucharistic table, all these threads are gathered. Memory and body, icon and song, liturgy and friendship, each woven into a sacramental whole. Here the Church does not merely remember but enacts doctrine as embodied hope and communal witness, where the grammar of divine love is broken and shared for the life of the world. Here, memory and future kiss; here, doctrine is broken and shared, becoming again the embodied witness of love, doctrine made flesh. The Spirit makes theology edible, communal, and radiant. The Church does not merely remember Christ; she is re-membered into Christ, becoming again what she receives: love poured out for the life of the world.

Doctrine, then, is not the Church's possession, but her vocation, the Spirit-formed, sacramentally enacted pedagogy that prepares the Church to live into God's future. It is the Spirit's choreography of a holy life, a life that echoes the music of heaven in the streets of earth. It is lived not in isolation but in communion, not through speculation but through incarnation, a life formed in icons and Eucharist, in friendship and witness, in song and sacrament. It forms disciples who see with the eyes of mercy, sing with the voice of praise, serve with the hands of Christ, and live in the rhythm of Triune love.

This is doctrine made flesh. This is formation for God's future.

Chapter Six
Doctrine in the Wild
The Faithful Grammar of Love in a Fractured World and God's Future

As John and Charles Wesley have often described, we are "transcripts of the Trinity" (Wesley). Formed by that image of Triune love, we are sent out into the wild as were Moses and Jesus, at the behest of the Spirit, to write our stories of faith with the grammar of God's love that is already etched in the fabric of the universe as the Wisdom of the Creator, for the life of the world. Not only does our future and all things of creation depend upon this unfolding faithful storytelling of New Creation's inbreaking, but God's future is wrapped up with our surprising narratives of faithful witness and eschatological hope. When our doctrine(s), our stories of faith become flesh in the wild, then we script the grammar of God's love with the yearning of creation that prepares God's future and ours in the New Creation.

As the whole creation groans to see the face of God, the Spirit sighs deeply for creations' full imagining. Keep listening to the Spirit, and we will hear from the depths that all shall be well even amid darkness and that God is always at home, inviting us into divine presence through stillness and surrender, the Triune Creator yearning with anticipation and desire to behold God's own 'new face' shining in the face of all things of creation. This is how we learn to write our stories of faith in the wild with the grammar of God's infinite vulnerable love. This is doxology written in every nook and cranny of creation to the "finish of New Creation" (Charles Wesley) that is as endless and everlasting as the infinite vulnerable love that is God.

Framing the Chapter
The Future That Beckons

This final chapter gathers the threads of memory, embodiment, and public witness into a vision of ecclesial formation grounded in hope. The Church does not merely remember doctrine or perform it in the wild, she is being formed by it into the shape of God's future, shaped precisely through the unpredictable, contexts where faith is tested and love must act. Doctrine, made flesh in the life of the Church, becomes a pathway of spiritual maturity, communal discernment, and mission in a fractured world, marked by cultural dislocation, ecological crisis, and political unrest.

To speak of formation is to ask: how is doctrine shaping who we are becoming? What kind of people are we being made into by the stories we rehearse, the sacraments we receive, and the witness we bear? This is not merely a pastoral concern, but a theological imperative. For doctrine, if true, is not static but kinetic, it draws us forward into the life of the Triune God, into the making of all things new.

The Church, therefore, must not only be rooted in memory and resilient in witness, but also animated by eschatological imagination. She is not the curator of old truths, but the crucible in which new creation is rehearsed, anticipated, and lived, a crucible fired by the resurrection's first light and shaped by the Spirit's promise of all things made new. The Kin-dom of God is not an empty metaphor. It is a future that has already begun, a future whose first light has already dawned in the resurrection of Christ.

Doctrine lived in the wild is not only faithful to the past but prophetic toward God's promised future. It is rooted in memory and risen in hope, walking toward the New Creation where all things are being made new. If memory is the Church's soil and embodiment its flowering, then this chapter traces the fruit: doctrine lived in public, in pain, in pluralism, and in perseverance. This is the missionary overflow of tradition that has been remembered and transfigured. It is the path doctrine takes when it leaves the sanctuary and enters the world's wild places. This is no departure from orthodoxy but its truest expression, for the Triune God is abundant outpouring love. The Father sends, the Son embodies, and the Spirit empowers. The Church, shaped by this divine choreography, is sent into the wild, not to dominate the world but to faithfully dwell in it, not to escape the world but to engage it. Doctrine, if it is to be faithful, must move with this same centrifugal energy of love. The creation's groaning depends on our faithful grammar of love that is learning from eschatological hope: that is, hope shaped by God's promised future, breaking into the present through the resurrection, compelling us to live as if new creation is already underway.

Doctrine on the Street: Public Faith in a Fragmented Age

Where might you walk doctrine today? Who needs to hear the good news not in debate but in bread, not in argument but in presence? What happens when doctrine leaves the sanctuary? When it walks outside the nave into a world torn by injustice, consumerism, violence, and despair? Doctrine that is sung in the liturgy must be lived in the marketplace. It cannot remain confined to the sanctuary's echo. If it is to be true, it must take on shoes.

Doctrine on the street is not stripped of reverence but infused with urgency. It becomes lived theology, a public faith that speaks with both tenderness and boldness into the fractured places of human experience. It proclaims Christ not as an abstraction but as the crucified and risen one who walks alongside the hungry, the oppressed, and the weary. It is not doctrine detached from mystery, but doctrine enfleshed in mercy. Prophetic doctrine is no weapon, it is a wound, borne in love for both truth and the Church which it seeks to heal.

True doctrine is born not in conquest but in *kenosis*, in the emptying that makes space for God to be born in the soul. This resonates with the Christ hymn of Philippians 2, where Christ empties himself in radical love. On the street, this kenotic doctrine becomes a presence that listens before it speaks, welcomes before it warns, and walks alongside rather than ahead. Theology of this sort holds the world's brokenness in the light of divine patience, not fleeing it but bearing it with radiant trust. This radical trust in divine love resonates deeply with the vision of doctrine in the wild, as a grammar of love that persists through chaos, bearing witness to God's eschatological faithfulness even when history seems fatally shattered.

In a world increasingly dominated by ideology and polarizing slogans, doctrine can degenerate into mere identity signaling, a badge of tribalistic belonging or a weapon of exclusion of ecclesial apartheid. But faithful doctrine resists that impulse. It bears witness to a deeper allegiance: to the Triune God whose love exceeds tribalism, nationalism, and reductionism. The Church must learn to speak again not with weapons, but with wounds; not to dominate, but to dwell, following the nonviolent witness of Jesus, who bore suffering without retaliation and offered peace in the very place of violence.

This kind of public doctrine does not rush to explain; it listens. It does not overpower; it accompanies. It recognizes that truth is not simply something to be asserted, but something to be shared, embodied, and practiced in community. Doctrine, then, is not merely what the Church proclaims for herself in safety; it is what she suffers in solidarity for the life of the world.

The Church that bears Chirist's name must follow in that pattern: speaking faith in the public square not as ideology, but as love made visible. To proclaim Christ in this age is to embody doctrine with courage and compassion in the public arena. It is to say, with word and gesture: God's Beloved Kin-dom is near, even here, even now.

By "God's Beloved Kin-dom," we name the spacious, Spirit-born reality that rises from the ashes of exile and death, a divine household of justice and joy. This is oikodome, God's broad and generous dwelling, the makom of Hebrew imagination and the promise of Christ: not merely a physical space, but a revelation of God's own expansive, vulnerable love. The Church as the living Body of Christ is both promise and presence of this kin-dom, where every stranger is kin, every wound becomes a witness, and all creation is being gathered into the household of God, renewed, reconciled, and resurrected. Amen.

The Cross in the Marketplace: Suffering and Solidarity

Embodied doctrine is never abstract. It walks the way of the cross. In the marketplace of power, spectacle, and self-interest, Christian witness must bear the marks of the Crucified. If doctrine is to mean anything in public, it must be cruciform: shaped by suffering love, marked by vulnerability, and driven by mercy.

The marketplace in the ancient world was not simply a center for commerce; it was the seat of public discourse, political spectacle, and imperial control. It was there that Jesus was paraded, mocked, and condemned. The public square has always been a space of visibility and judgment. To speak doctrine there is to risk exposure, misunderstanding, and sometimes, rejection. But it is also the space where God has already gone before.

The mystics speak of this movement downward, into hiddenness, loss, and divine solidarity. The Body of Christ broken and shared in the sanctuary must lead to the Body of Christ carried and broken in the world, a *Eucharistic missio*, commissioning the Church to become what it receives and to risk what it proclaims. Doctrine, shaped by the Table, prepares the Church to be poured out. It is not merely what is said in communion, but what is risked in community.

The cross in the marketplace is not only a confrontation with the powers of the world, but also a commissioning, animated by the mystical theology that fuels prophetic public action. It offers a pattern of holy courage. The voices of the mystics remind us that doctrine shaped by contemplative depths becomes prophetic embodiment, truth that walks, weeps, and wounds in love for the world. It engages the powers of the world, it commissions us into the work of peace, justice, and mercy. When doctrine is shaped by suffering love, it becomes a public grammar of healing. The Body of Christ, broken and poured out, is no mere symbol, it is the pattern for a Church that is willing to be broken for the life of the world. This is where public theology finds its power: not in institutional preservation, but in cruciform witness, formed by the Eucharistic grammar of self-giving love and public hope. As we move toward creation's groaning and glory, we carry forward a doctrine that dares to weep, walk, and work in love. The marketplace becomes the meeting ground of grace. The street becomes sacred ground, preparing us for the voice of creation crying out with the hope of new birth.

Creation as Catechesis: Ecological Discipleship
Spiritual Practice: Earthbound Discipleship

Once a week, go outside without agenda. Leave your phone. Leave your books. Listen for one hour to the world's liturgy: the song of wind, the hymn of leaves, the silent sermon of stone and sky. Breathe the air as benediction. Touch the soil as sacred. Let doctrine be heard not only in creeds, but in the symphony of creation. Then return to your life changed, not above the world, but within it. Not apart from creation, but as part of its praise.

Theological Reflection: Creation, the First Sacrament

Creation is not merely our dwelling place; it is our first catechism, the sacred ground where we learn to love, to trust, and to behold. Before there were creeds, there were rivers. Before there were doctrines, there were stars. The earth is not simply our habitat, it is the first sacrament of God's making, the place where divine presence pulses through leaf and light, soil and sky. Doctrine comes alive when it is rooted in this sacred soil.

St. Bonaventure describes creation as the mirror and footprint (*vestigium*) of the Trinity. Each creature, he taught, reflects the divine beauty and reveals a path of ascent into the heart of God. Such sacramental cosmology invites a participatory and contemplative way of knowing, an ascent that begins in wonder and leads to union. Thus, the world is not a distraction from theology, it is its very ground and invitation.

Julian of Norwich once reflected on a simple hazelnut, an image that, when linked to the Eucharistic imagination, reveals how even the smallest created thing participates in the fullness of divine love and sustenance shown to her in a vision. Holding it in her hand, she hears God say: "It lasts and ever shall, because God loves it." The entire cosmos is held in God's intimate, sustaining grace.

Nothing is too small to be sacred. Creation itself is doctrine whispered in green and gold.

Creation is not a static text but a living teacher, one that reflects the wisdom, power and goodness of the Creator and like doctrine, speaks with a dynamic grammar, always unfolding into deeper communion with the divine. The cosmos is not closed or finished but in perpetual movement, an epektasis, or infinite ascent, drawing all creation ever more deeply into God's inexhaustible beauty. This vision of creation as a school of love and mystery suggests that doctrine, too, must remain dynamic and open, formed through contemplative discernment and ecological encounter within the world God so lovingly sustains. To embrace this vision is to recognize that faithful doctrine is not frozen in time but moves with the Spirit's breath across the living world, guiding the Church into ever-deepening participation in the divine life.

Psalm 19 proclaims, "The heavens declare the glory of God; the skies proclaim the work of his hands." Romans 8 tells us that creation groans in labor pains, awaiting the revealing of the children of God. These are not metaphors, they are reminders that the natural world is both sacramental and eschatological, signs that reveal divine presence and future fulfillment. The Church cannot profess faith in the Creator while ignoring the cries of creation. To do so is to sever sacramental ethics from ecological fidelity, for the Eucharistic pattern already established in worship compels us to attend to the suffering and redemption of all creation as integral to the Church's faithful witness.

An ecological discipleship is not a political preference but a spiritual posture. It means living now as if new creation were already breaking in, because it is. It means treating the doctrine of creation not as a distant doctrine of origin, but as an active grammar of love written into the fabric of forests, tides, clouds, and creatures. It is to hear the world not as background noise but as divine testimony.

To reclaim our place in creation is not to rise above it, but to kneel within it. Creation is not a stage for salvation; it is a partner in God's story. When we bless the land, protect the waters, and listen to the wind, we are not only stewarding resources, but we are also participating in God's renewal of all things. This stewardship is not ancillary to salvation; it is bound to God's future and our own.

In caring for creation, we rehearse our hope: that the same Spirit who hovered over the waters in Genesis is still breathing new life into a groaning world. In this way, creation does not simply point to God, it places us within God's unfolding song and life. The Creation is God's way of being God, an expression echoed in the theological vision of Bonaventure, who saw all of creation as *vestigium Dei*, and Julian of Norwich, who beheld divine love sustaining even a hazelnut. Creation and the Creator are indissolubly bound, not by necessity, but by the gracious overflow of infinite vulnerable love.

The trees and tides, stars and soil, are all part of a living liturgy, one that proclaims both the goodness of beginnings and the nearness of a redeemed future. Faithful doctrine, the grammar of the Creator's love and joy over the goodness of creation, rooted in this sacred ground becomes a form of eschatological witness, echoing Romans 8 and the Spirit's ongoing creation, and in this sacred ground becomes a living witness to the hope that creation itself will be transfigured in love.

Embodied Doctrine Across Cultures

Doctrine does not come to us in a single language, melody, or skin, it flows from the generous hospitality of Pentecost, a revelation of the Trinity's relational plenitude that embraces difference without dissolving communion. Cultural diversity, in this sense, mirrors creation's own polyphony, echoing the varied beauty of the world God made and loves. It emerges from Pentecost, a miracle of many tongues, many ears, many hearts. The Church is catholic not because it is uniform, but because it is capacious, wide enough to embrace and be enriched by the many ways faith takes flesh in the world.

Pentecost, as described in Acts 2, is not simply the origin of Christian proclamation, it is the divine validation of cultural particularity. The Spirit speaks in the native languages of all gathered. Doctrine, from its first breath, is multilingual, polyphonic, and incarnational. What is not assumed is not healed, emphasizing that the Spirit's redemptive work enters fully into the scandalous particularity of culture, healing from within. The Word becomes flesh anew in every time and place, underscoring that sound doctrine, the faithful grammar of love, is not monolithic but must be continually incarnated and contextualized. These early theological insights reveal that doctrinal faithfulness requires cultural embodiment, they connect divine revelation to the dynamic, living fabric of human diversity. Doctrine does not demand sameness; it celebrates communion in difference. What would the unitive love of God be without difference?

Every aspect of creation, every face, every culture, every language, every particle, reveals a hidden facet of God. We are not merely neighbors; we are kin to all that exists, from stardust to soil, from breath to branch. Ours is a belonging that transcends species, elements, and epochs, a communion not only of humanity, but of all that shares in the dance of creation.

Doctrine must be spacious enough to make room for this radical kinship, a grammar of grace capacious enough to echo in every quark of reality, binding the cosmos into a single, sacred chorus of belonging.

José Míguez Bonino speaking from the heart of Latin American liberation theology, echoes the prophetic witness of Amos and Isaiah by declaring that "Theology in Latin America begins with the cry of the poor." Doctrine, therefore, must be accountable not to empire or abstraction, but to the lived experiences of those who suffer. The gospel sounds different among the oppressed, and doctrine, if it is faithful, will bend its ear to their cry.

John Dominic Crossan, in *Render unto Caesar*, challenges us to reread Scripture not through imperial lenses, but through the eyes of the crucified. In his reading, Jesus' statement "Render unto Caesar" is not a call to passive citizenship, but a prophetic critique of the violent machinery of empire. Doctrine across cultures must be honest about its historical complicities and courageous in its liberative reimagining. Otherwise, doctrine will function as the law that led to Jesus' death, it will obstruct God's justice and fail to be the faith that speaks with the grammar of God's love.

To embody doctrine in a multicultural world is to relinquish control and embrace communion. No one culture exhausts the truth of the gospel, but each bears a facet of its fullness. This is Pentecostal doctrine, spoken in many tongues, borne on wind and fire, fire-shaped and Spirit-filled, announcing that God's truth reverberates in every voice willing to sing grace into the world. It is the Church learning again what it means to be one, holy, catholic, and apostolic, not in sameness, but in the stunning mosaic of love.

Embodied doctrine across cultures means recognizing that theology wears different garments in different places. It dances to different rhythms, feeds on different harvests, grieves in different rituals, and sings in different keys. This is not relativism; it is reverent plurality, a posture that honors cultural diversity while upholding the theological integrity of the gospel. It is the conviction that the Spirit does not clone but creates. Doctrine, then, is not a static set of ideas imposed on the world, but a living tradition woven through global testimonies of grace.

To be faithful to doctrine in this era is to practice a listening Church, a Church that learns as it teaches, receives as it gives, and weeps in languages not its own. The grammar of God's love must be spoken with many accents, anticipating the unity-in-difference of the New Creation, a Pentecostal vision where diversity is not erased but fulfilled in shared praise, shaped by many stories, and sung in many tones. This is the sound of Pentecost still echoing through the world. This is the wild music of divine communion.

Toward a Theology of Embodied Resilience

In an age of exhaustion, anxiety, and fragmentation, the Church is called not only to embody hope but to sustain it. Doctrine in the wild must be more than declarative; it must be resilient. It must nourish the soul in dry seasons, sustain justice in hostile places, and hold communities together when ecclesial life frays and societal bonds collapse, when the center no longer holds.

Embodied resilience is not the refusal to feel fatigue. It is the grace to stand again when the song falters and the light dims, fortified by the Spirit who sustains our breath, restores our strength, and accompanies us in the shadows. It is rooted not in human determination but in divine faithfulness. It draws breath from the Spirit who groans within us and strength from the One who bore the cross and rose with scars.

This kind of resilience sings lament and alleluia in the same breath. It teaches the Church to walk with the slow, to rest with the weary, to grieve with those who mourn, and to act with holy defiance against every form of death.

The Eucharist, in this light, becomes our curriculum of resilience: a table where woundedness is not hidden, but gathered; where justice is remembered not only in words, but in the sharing of bread and cup. Here, the Church rehearses the grammar of survival, not as retreat from the world, but as preparation to re-enter it with courage shaped by communion.

From this eucharistic rehearsal emerges a deeper capacity for doctrinal maturity. Doctrine shaped in this furnace of love becomes not brittle dogma but flexible fidelity, formed by communion, tested through suffering, and responsive to cultural plurality. It embodies the evolving grammar of faith that endures not by rigidity, but by its capacity to love faithfully in changing and fractured contexts, capable of bending with sorrow, enduring in joy, and bearing the weight of the world's brokenness without breaking apart. This is not doctrinal minimalism; it is doctrinal maturity. It is what happens when love is learned in adversity and spoken through wounds.

To be resilient is not merely to persist, but to love again and again. To trust that what is sown in weakness will be raised in glory. To speak the name of Jesus not as a slogan, but as breath shared in the communion of saints, the fellowship of the suffering, and the company of those who still believe that the world can be made new.

This is the wild grammar of resurrection hope. This is doctrine, still breathing, still burning, still becoming flesh.

And so, we turn now, from vision to vocation. Having traced the Spirit's movement across wilderness and wounds, we pause to ask: how might doctrine be lived, embodied, and practiced amid the fractures of our world? What does this grammar of hope look like when spoken with our lives? What follows are invitations for discernment, for practice, and for praise, ways to embody the doctrine we've received in the everyday liturgies of love.

Practicing Doctrine in the Wild: A Connexional Praxis of Love

Where is our doctrine most at risk of becoming abstraction?

How can we embody our tradition in public love, not just private piety?

Who are the "strangers" we are called to see, serve, and stand beside?

In what ways can Valarie Kaur's call to "Revolutionary Love" and John Wesley's "Methodist Practice of Connexion" shape our community's mission in the world?

The Church's vocation is not to curate doctrine in a vault, but to enact what John Wesley called 'practical divinity', a Spirit-choreographed testimony to Trinitarian grace in motion, but to carry it as bread. As John Wesley envisioned, connexion is not a static institution but a Spirit-choreographed movement of relational grace, a living network of mutual aid, shared witness, and faithful risk. In Wesley's practice of connexion, we glimpse a hopeful ecclesiology: a Church formed not by power, but by proximity; not by conformity, but by charity.

This is where doctrine breathes, in the seams of shared burdens, in the touch of healing hands, in the feet that walk toward suffering. The faithful grammar of God's love, when shaped by connexional witness, becomes an embodied song across generations and geographies. In this wild harmony, the Church becomes an icon of God's future.

Liturgical Reflection: A Table of Resilient Love
Call and Response for Eucharistic Resilence

Leader: When we falter, when we fear, when we are weary.
People: Feed us again with the bread of endurance.
Leader: When love costs us comfort, and justice calls us to risk.
People: Pour us out with the wine of courage.
Leader: Where the world wounds, and sorrow lingers.
People: Bind us together as the Body of Christ.
Leader: For every broken heart, for every trembling hope.
People: Teach us again the grammar of grace.
All: Let this Table form us in faith, that we may rise in love and walk in wild resilience.

Closing Prayer
God of crucified glory and risen grace,
You have called us not to silence, but to song;
Not to isolation, but to incarnation;
Not to survive, but to love.
Root our doctrine not in defense, but in daring.
Shape our hearts not with answers, but with communion.
Break us, bless us, and send us, as living witnesses of your abundant, wild, and wounded love.
In the name of the One who walked the streets, bore the cross, broke the bread, and breathes still in the weary.
Amen.

From the table we rise, not as individuals inspired, but as a people sent. What has been prayed in communion, we now live in community. Doctrine, when shaped by worship, is not theory but testimony, faith rehearsed in love and offered back to the world. The conclusion that follows gathers this witness and breathes it forward, not as a closing, but as the Spirit's open-ended commission to become the doctrine we proclaim.

Conclusion: Living Doctrine, Breathing Glory

Doctrine is not a possession to be defended. It is a witness to be lived, testifying to a grammar of love and breathing glory, to the crucified and risen Christ in every act of love, every breath of protest, and every tear of hope. Doctrine is not the subject; it is the syntax and grammar of Faith. The Church does not live by doctrine alone but through the faith that writes that code of love into our hearts. Faith, energized by divine love, searches always for the language, practices, and pathways to embody that love. Doctrine is not a system we preserve but a code we enact, a lived grammar that embodies faith in holy communion with the world's pain and God's promise. As with syntax in language, doctrine orders our witness and enables coherent expression; it is not the end, but the structure through which love speaks and acts faithfully in the world.

To live doctrine in this world is to be drawn deeper into the triune life of God, into the vulnerable love of the Son, the groaning power of the Spirit, and the generous heart of the Father. It thrives on the Spirit's presence in flesh and blood, breath and bread, fracture and fire.

At the Table, we are not only fed but formed. We are given to one another, sent to one another, broken for the life of the world. The Church's doctrine, when rooted in this meal, is never a system of belief but a choreography of grace. It teaches us how to kneel, how to carry each other, how to sing even when breath is scarce.

This is the apocalyptic vocation of doctrine in a fractured world: to unveil the hidden glory, to bear the wounds of love, to resist despair with resurrection breath. Doctrine becomes what it was always meant to be: the living memory of divine love, carried forward in hope.

Doctrine, when it is alive, will look like bread passed between hands, oil poured out on wounds, protest songs in city streets, and stories told around sacred fires. It will look like Christ among us.

And it will sound, again and again, like the Spirit whispering: "Behold, I am making all things new."

Epilogue
A Cautionary Tale

When the Church forgets that doctrine is born of prayer and meant to express the love of God, she risks turning means of grace into instruments of control. And when doctrine becomes detached from love, it no longer opens the heart to God, it closes the door to others.

The grammar of love that runs with the grain of the universe is the very Wisdom of God. The Wisdom of the Spirit will always lead and guide us with the truth that faithful doctrine attempts to speak: God is love, infinite vulnerable love from everlasting to everlasting. As we are awakened with the knowledge that we are known and loved with the infinite vulnerable love of God, the Wisdom of the Creator is awakened in us, and we are filled with joyous gratitude, grace and profound humility. This way of knowing love in the world is too wonderful to be contained in any container of ecclesial certainty. Certainty is idolatry. It is the breeding ground of narrow, defensive dogmatism that mistakes control and exclusion for faith. When the posture of the Church takes up doctrine as the grammar of certainty, it begins to wield doctrines of certainty: such as the doctrine of hell and the doctrine of original sin, as weapons to control and exclude with the idols of certainty.

We have seen this happen before.

In 1493, the Papal Bull known as the Doctrine of Discovery declared that any land not inhabited by Christians could be claimed by Christian powers. Issued under the banner of Christ, it proclaimed that "the Catholic faith and the Christian religion be exalted and be everywhere increased and spread, that the health of souls be cared for and that barbarous nations be overthrown and brought to the faith itself." This grievous doctrine gave theological justification for the domination of Indigenous peoples and later became one of the foundational rationales for the transatlantic slave trade. What began as a baptized assertion of theological truth became a mechanism for colonialism, conquest, and erasure. When doctrine is untethered from love, it becomes not a channel of grace but a source of grave injustice, not only for human beings but for all things of creation.

When the Church loses the memory of how her faith was forged in prayer, in tears, in longing, in song, she begins to preserve doctrine not as testimony but as weapon that will be used against all things of creation. She forgets that her truest doctrines were first whispered in awe and love, not shouted in exclusion and control.

This is why St. Francis of Assisi taught that the earth, the trees, the animals, the stars, speak the language of praise without words. Long before the Church ever codified doctrine, or canonized Scripture and forged the Creeds, creation was already singing, the whole creation already knows the grammar of love. When the Church forgets this, she forgets her place in the choir of creation.

Without the whole of creation we have no access to God, for creation itself is the medium through which the divine is revealed. Without the witness of creation, we lose not only the capacity to see God, we lose the very capacity to be fully human. Creation is hardwired with the grammar of love. The very Word that spoke creation into existence by the breath of God's mouth is the Wisdom of the Creator (Proverbs 8) that creates a world drenched with the Wisdom of She who is, the Spirit who pours the energy of God's love into and over all of the Creator's works.

This future is not simply creation's hope, it is God's own. God's future is bound up with creation's renewal, and creation's flourishing is the joy of God's fulfillment.

And as Simone Weil teaches, true knowledge begins with attention. "Attention is the rarest and purest form of generosity," she wrote in *Waiting for God*. When we cease to be attentive, to God, to our neighbor, to the poor, to the wounded creation, we begin to speak falsely, especially when our creeds are used as if they remain permanently fixed. We forget that the creeds were never meant to close minds, but to open hearts, hearts attuned to a love that is always unfolding, always leading us further into the mystery of God.

Doctrine divorced from attention becomes a language of faith that is without compassion. But there is another way, and this book has been a journey toward it. Doctrine that is breathed into being through the Spirit, formed in prayer, tested in the fires of love, and opened in hope will always bend toward life. We do not need to reject doctrine. We need to remember how to pray it. We need to learn again how to listen, to speak in the language of love.

All doctrine, then, must be oriented toward this future: a living hope that is already breathing into the present. The Spirit is not only the source of life but the one who draws all of creation into the deifying love of God. Creation itself is invited into communion, not as backdrop, but as participant.

When the Church forgets this future-oriented hope, her doctrines grow cold. But when she remembers, her doctrines become songs of new creation, sacraments of transformation, echoes of the joy that is coming, and, in the Christ, already here.

A Concluding Blessing and Promise

To all who have walked this journey through faith and doctrine, let this work be a word of blessing:

May your faith be ever rooted in prayer, awakened by love, and stretched as wide and deep and high as the infinite vulnerable love of God that is from everlasting to everlasting.

May you listen deeply to the Spirit's groans in all creation; for in the Spirit's deepest sighs, too deep for words, you will hear from "deep calling to deep" the invitation to go where healing, hope, and peace are needed most.

Listen to the Spirit bringing the Creator near to you. And remember even Scripture cannot contain the fullness of God's infinite, vulnerable love. Yet it remains a means of grace, the Spirit's gift for helping us listen across the ages and remember who we are, and whose we are, as we come from God and return home to God.

Listen to creation. This is the place where the Creator dwells and this is the place where you and all things of creation share in the glory and love of the Creator. And this is the place where you will meet with joy the fulfillment of the Creator's hope and desire and all creation's longing to dance in eternal joy in the household of God.

Listen to the saints and strangers around you. Offer the joy of hospitality to all things of creation and be prepared to be surprised by joy, just as the Creator was overcome with ecstatic joy when the Word first spoke the world into being.

And may all our faithful work at learning how to speak the words of love surprise even God again, as all creation returns home, not with the same borrowed words of past generations, but with new ones, filled with the kind of doxology and love that birthed creation into being.

May your doctrines never harden into stones of exclusion but remain as living testimonies, cracked open by awe, warmed by compassion, and transfigured by hope.

Let your faithful memory be tender. Let your vision be wide and soft. And may your trust be fearless so your love may grow as infinite and vulnerable as the One who is by nature infinite vulnerable love.

For the One who is Love will not leave you comfortless and without a guide. The One who promised is faithful to see that we reach our end where we may begin to speak as faithfully as the One who is Love.

"The Spirit will not let us miss providence's way," declares Charles Wesley. And, as Elizabeth Johnson taught us, She Who Is, the Spirit, the Lord and giver of life, is the One who enables the Creator to speak the Word by the breath of God's mouth and suffuse into every nook and cranny of the Creation, the Wisdom of the Creator. Yes, this Spirit who leads and guides all creation along the path in the Way, the Truth, and the Life of the Word that spoke creation into existence is the same good Word that became flesh and continues to hold all things of creation together in his Body. She Who Is, the Wisdom of creation (Proverbs 8) is always faithful to "stir up good trouble" (John Lewis) until we are awakened to the Wisdom of the infinite vulnerable love of the Creator from everlasting to everlasting: "when we rise in love renewed, we will resemble an image of the Triune God through all eternity" (Charles Wesley).

The promise of the promise keeper is this: God will be all in all, and the infinite vulnerable love that is God will have the final Word to our faithful grammar of love.

And so, as we began this book in prayer, let us close this book in prayer alongside the ancient Christian Prayer:

Come Holy Spirit and kindle in us the fire of your love.
Lord, we trust you! Heal our unbelief that keeps clinging to all those idolatrous beliefs of certainty.
Take our minds and think through them.
Awaken and renew our minds with the mind of Christ that we may trust you with the faith and faithfulness of our Lord.
Take our lips and speak through them.
Give to us the faith that speaks with the Wisdom of all creation the grammar of Love.
Now, take our souls and set them on fire.
Fill us with the energy of your infinite vulnerable love that is from everlasting to everlasting.
Amen.
Thanks be to God.
Soli Deo gloria!

Postlude
Do No Harm

This book was written in the wake of my defrocking a few years after my retirement from the church tradition in which I was ordained for forty years. I choose not to name the denomination here. To do so would distract from the spirit of this book, which seeks not to wound, but to witness, to offer a grammar of love that speaks truth in mercy, and mercy with clarity. My aim is to do no harm. But love does not mean silence. To love is to speak truthfully, in faith, with the voice God has given you.

For four decades I taught the faith and the faithfulness of Christ, proclaiming the Gospel as good news for all creation. I gave my life to nurturing doctrine as a living, breathing witness to God's unfolding future, doctrine as a Spirit-shaped language of grace, not a weapon of control. I taught in four educational institutions from my very young church tradition, still in its infancy, just beginning its second century of trying to figure out what it means to be the Church catholic and how to faithfully navigate faith and doctrine and infinite vulnerable love. I have been trying to show that doctrine is not fixed or universally the same in all times and places. Doctrine is a song of the Spirit, rising from the energy of God's infinite vulnerable love, a love that groans and sighs through history and in every quark of reality, ever drawing us toward New Creation.

Eventually, this vision, so long nurtured and so clearly grounded in the Church catholic, was no longer welcomed. And so, my ordination was taken. But even in that grief, I do not raise my voice in anger. This book is not my defense. The best defense is to trust the infinite vulnerable love of God. It is a labor of love, an offering, a witness, a seed sown for the sake of those who are coming.

And they are coming. For forty years, I stood and sat before the faces of thousands of students, fresh voices from God's future. They came with questions, wonder, resistance, longing. In them, I saw the God of our future arriving. As I looked into their eyes, I saw promise and disillusionment. Often the disillusion was the dissonance of what they see in the world, in their church traditions, and what they glimpsed from the future they had come. As a promise from God, I saw the faith of Christ taking on new flesh, a grammar of love being formed anew. They were speaking a language of love straight from the future. New Creation kept coming through them. What I have seen in them I cannot unsee; what I have heard, I cannot unhear.

So, pay attention to them. Listen to the Spirit breathing through their lives. They will take your breath away, and give you back your future.

A Word to My Students
Speaking in the Grammar of Love

To my students who have felt confused, disoriented, or even alienated by the Church's doctrines: let me say again what I have always said to you: pay attention to the infinite vulnerable love of God that lives in you. The Spirit that pulses and breathes in you is the breath of God. Breathe deeply and speak from that place. Speak the grammar of love that is already alive in you waiting to be told. Tell your story, not just another form of someone else's story. Let no ecclesial institution rob you of your voice; they need to hear your ways of seeing as much as you need to stay connected to them.

Remember, the wisdom that thrums through the universe is the Word, the *Logos*, who became flesh and dwelt among us, full of grace and truth. Astonishingly, this Word is not an idea, or concept, or category. The infinite vulnerable love that is God is always more than any idea of our imagination. This living breathing creating Word is a Person. And the only way to know the Truth that is the Word is to be encountered by the infinite vulnerable love of God.

As John Milbank has said, when you hear the Word Made Strange, you must respond with your own word, or you have not yet heard at all.

Lisa Isherwood echoes this insight: we must learn to "queer the Scriptures." To queer is to notice what is strange, original, and unsettling in love and then speak with our own queer voices for the rest of the world to hear. Since each of us is an original, unrepeatable image of the Trinity, distinct yet formed in relational unity, our speech must be likewise unique as the voice of Father, Son and Holy Spirit.

We must speak not only about God, but from within the life of God, in voices that resonate with the unrepeatable music of our own being. God yearns to hear our newest voices as much as we yearn to hear God's. Together, and surprisingly, we are participating in the making of all things new in New Creation.

Now, here is my point: for the life of the world, let the infinite vulnerable love of God push out your fears and give you the courage of love to speak from your uniquely original and unrepeatable voice, a strangely new, a queer word of love, to stretch and expand our minds and imagination to make room in our hearts for God's future and for all of creation.

Nearly a century ago, Alfred North Whitehead warned of the "fallacy of misplaced concreteness," mistaking our limited experience or language for universal truth. The Vincentian Canon, "everywhere, always, and by all," is not a historical achievement but an eschatological hope. Too often, churches have presumed their voice to be the universal one, silencing all others. But the Wisdom of God who became flesh and now holds all creation together is already speaking in a cacophony of voices. We must listen.

And remember: Pentecost was a cacophony. Many voices, many tongues, all aflame with the Spirit. It was disorienting, queer, strange, and some thought they were drunk. When the language of New Creation arrives, it always sounds bizarre to those who hear it for the first time.

To imitate Christ is not enough. We must speak Christ anew. Only when we speak from the fire that has touched our lips will we begin to speak anew with the grammar of infinite vulnerable love. Even Jesus said we would do greater things than he. That promise is not arrogance, it is the surprising joy of a God who delights in our voices.

James McClendon once titled a book, *Biography as Theology*, reflecting how our stories shape our vision and theological voice. God tells God's story through our lives. The silencing of those stories is a wound to the Spirit. What led to my defrocking was precisely this conviction, that faithful doctrine must be born again in every voice, in every generation, in every language. These fresh stories from New Creation are how the Church lives into the promise of God's future, and all of creations future.

Simiarily, Roberta Bondi's *To Pray and to Love* taught me this valuable pedagogy of storytelling. As a patristics scholar and spiritual theologian, she came to see that the faith of the church fathers and mothers is best taught through story. And so, she began to teach theology through narrative, because our stories are God's story being told. That insight reshaped my teaching and confirmed what I had long intuited: faithful doctrine as the grammar of God's love takes on flesh in our lived lives.

John Wesley, ever the theologian of *Theologia Practica*, reminded us that faith, hope, and love must not only be spoken, they must take root in the soil of creation. Doctrine is not an abstraction floating above the world. It is a seed sown in the dirt of our lives, watered by tears, awakened by Spirit. Wesley knew what the mystics knew: perfect love casts out fear, because perfect love enters flesh.

And yet, the institutional Church has often severed creation from new creation, as if heaven and hell were far-off places instead of present realities breaking in. From that idolatrously certain dichotomy it becomes easy to say: "You do not belong." For example, when the institutional Church bifurcates heaven from earth, as if to say future glory awaits you in heaven if you conform to our way of seeing and speaking and believing. These false dichotomies weaponize fear, silencing voices with the threat of hell.

In other words, when we pivot away from the original goodness of creation and presume that all of creation hinges on the Fall of creation and the original sinfulness of everyone made in the image of God, then it is easy to construct a pseudo-dualistic system of belief that says: Believe and you shall belong.

But the Good News of Christ says that all belong. Our belonging is not predicated upon our belief. We belong to God because God loves us. We do not believe to belong to God. The Faith of the Gospel declares what Christ taught us to pray: that God's Beloved Kin-dom is on earth as in heaven. Everything belongs because there is no separation, no divide, no us and them, in the household (*oikodome*) of God. All are drawn into the love of God. This is the constant refrain of all the mystics. Nicholas of Cusa wrote: "The machine of the world will have its center everywhere and its circumference nowhere, because its center and circumference are God, who is everywhere and nowhere." Similarly, Evelyn Underhill reminds us that God is infinite love, the center of everything and the circumference of nothing.

This is the essence of the Church's faith: to bear witness and partake of the infinite vulnerable love of God from everlasting to everlasting.

So, I leave you with this: Do no harm. But do not be silent. Speak your word. Tell your story. Respond faithfully to the Word made flesh in you with your strangely new and queer words of love that are becoming flesh in the future glory of New Creation.

And may the Spirit, "She Who is," Wisdom, breath, fire, and joy, set your heart ablaze with a grammar of love that is faithful, strange, and gloriously alive and totally surprising to the Creator and all that God has made. Amen.

A Selected Bibliography

Abraham, William J. 1998. *Canon and Criterion in Christian Theology: From the Fathers to Feminism*. Oxford: Oxford University Press.

Abraham, William J., Jason E. Vickers, and Natalie B. Van Kirk. 2008. *Canonical Theism: A Proposal for Theology and the Church*. Grand Rapids: Eerdmans.

Ayres, Lewis. 2004. *Nicaea and Its Legacy: An Approach to Fourth-Century Trinitarian Theology*. Oxford: Oxford University Press.

Balthasar, Hans Urs von. 2008. *Engagement with God: The Drama of Christian Discipleship*. San Francisco, California: Ignatius Press.

_____. 2004. *Love Alone Is Credible*. San Francisco: Ignatius Press.

_____. 1955. *Prayer*. San Francisco: Ignatius Press.

_____. 1983. *The Glory of the Lord a Theological Aesthetics.*: Vol. 1. *Seeing the Form*. San Francisco: Ignatius Press.

Bondi, Roberta C. 1987. *To Love as God Loves: Conversations with the Early Church*. Philadelphia: Fortress.

_____. 1991. *To Pray & to Love: Conversations on Prayer with the Early Church*. Minneapolis: Fortress.

Brueggemann, Walter, and Davis Hankins. 2018. *The Prophetic Imagination*. 40th anniversary edition. Minneapolis: Fortress.

Bromiley, Geoffrey William. 1978. *Historical Theology: An Introduction*. Grand Rapids: Eerdmans.

Catherine of Siena. *The Dialogue of Divine Providence*. (various translations).

Coakley, Sarah. 2013. *God, Sexuality and the Self: An Essay 'On the Trinity'*. Cambridge: Cambridge University Press.

_____. 2002. *Re-Thinking Gregory of Nyssa*. Malden, Mass.: Blackwell.

Coakley, Sarah. 2015. *The New Asceticism: Sexuality, Gender and the Quest for God*. London: Continuum.

Crossan, John Dominic. 2022. *Render unto Caesar: The Struggle over Christ and Culture in the New Testament*. First edition. New York, NY: Harper One.

Epp-Stobbe, Eleanor. 2000. "Practising God's Hospitality: The Contribution of Letty M. Russell toward an Understanding of the Mission of the Church." Dissertation: University of Toronto.

Gorman, Michael J. 2015. *Becoming the Gospel: Paul, Participation, and Mission*. Grand Rapids: Eerdmans.

_____. 2009. *Inhabiting the Cruciform God: Kenosis, Justification, and Theosis in Paul's Narrative Soteriology*. Grand Rapids: Eerdmans.

St. Gregory of Nyssa. 2002. *On God and Christ: The Five Theological Orations and Two Letters to Cledonius*. Trans. by Frederick Williams and Lionel R. Wickham. Crestwood, New York: St. Vladimir's Seminary Press.

_____. 1967. *Ascetical Works*. Trans. Virginia Woods Callahan. Washington, D.C.: Catholic University of America Press.

_____. 1978. *The Life of Moses*. San Francisco: Harper San Francisco.

_____. 2002. *On the Soul and the Resurrection*. Trans. Catharine Roth. Crestwood, N.Y: St. Vladimir's Seminary Press.

Hays, Christopher B., and Richard B. Hays. 2024. *The Widening of God's Mercy: Sexuality within the Biblical Story*. New Haven: Yale University Press.

Hays, Richard B. 2020. *Reading with the Grain of Scripture*. Grand Rapids: Eerdmans.

_____. 2014. *Reading Backwards: Figural Christology and the Fourfold Gospel Witness*. Waco, Texas: Baylor University Press.

Irenaeus. 1992. *Against the Heresies*. Edited by John J. Dillon (*et al.*). Trans. Dominic J. Unger. Ancient Christian Writers. New York: Newman Press.

Isherwood, Lisa, and Elaine Bellchambers. 2010. *Through Us, with Us, in Us: Relational Theologies in the Twenty-First Century*. London: SCM Press.

Jenson, Robert W. 2010. *Canon and Creed*. 1st ed. Louisville: Westminster/John Knox.

John of the Cross. 2012. *Collected Works of St. John of the Cross*. Memphis, TN: Bottom of the Hill Publishing.

Jennings, Willie James. 2020. *After Whiteness: An Education in Belonging*. Grand Rapids: Eerdmans.

Kaur, Valarie. 2020. *See No Stranger: A Memoir and Manifesto of Revolutionary Love*. New York: One World.

Kelly, J. N. D. 2003. *Early Christian Doctrines*. Rev. ed., Peabody, MA: Prince Press.

LaCugna, Catherine Mowry. 1991. *God for Us: The Trinity and Christian Life*. San Francisco: Harper San Francisco.

Lindbeck, George A. 2009. *The Nature of Doctrine: Religion and Theology in a Postliberal Age*. 25th anniversary ed. Louisville: Westminster/John Knox.

Lubac, Henri de, Susan Frank Parsons, and Laurence Paul Hemming. 2006. *Corpus Mysticum: The Eucharist and the Church in the Middle Ages: Historical Survey*. South Bend: University of Notre Dame Press.

McClendon, James Wm. 1990. *Biography as Theology: How Life Stories Can Remake Today's Theology*. New ed. Philadelphia: Trinity Press International.

Míguez Bonino, José. 1983. *Toward a Christian Political Ethics*. Philadelphia: Fortress.

Moltmann, Jürgen. 1977. *The Church in the Power of the Spirit: A Contribution to Messianic Ecclesiology*. Minneapolis: Fortress.

———. 2015. *The Crucified God*. 40th anniversary edition. Minneapolis: Fortress.

———. 2020. *The Spirit of Hope: Theology for a World in Peril*. Louisville: Presbyterian Publishing.

———. 1981. *The Trinity and the Kingdom: The Doctrine of God*. Minneapolis: Fortress.

Moltmann, Jürgen, and Margaret Kohl. 2004. *The Coming of God: Christian Eschatology*. Minneapolis: Fortress Press.

Newman, John Henry Cardinal. 2013. *An Essay on the Development Christian Doctrine*. Lanham: Start Publishing.

Julian of Norwich. (2022). *The Showings: Uncovering the Face of the Feminine in Revelations of Divine Love*. Trans. Richard Rohr. Charlottesville, VA: Hampton Roads.

Patterson, Stephen J. 2018. *The Forgotten Creed: Christianity's Original Struggle against Bigotry, Slavery, and Sexism*. Oxford: Oxford University Press.

Pelikan, Jaroslav. 1971. *The Christian Tradition: A History of the Development of Doctrine*. Chicago: University of Chicago Press.

Pelikan, Jaroslav. 1986. *The Vindication of Tradition*. New Haven: Yale University Press.

Placher, William C. 1994. *Narratives of a Vulnerable God: Christ, Theology, and Scripture*. 1st ed. Louisville: Westminster/John Knox.

Prestige, G. L. 1964. *God in Patristic Thought*. [2d ed.]. London: S.P.C.K.

Rahner, Karl. 1963. *The Church and the Sacraments*. New York: Herder and Herder.

———. 2001. *The Trinity*. Trans. J. F. Donceel. London: Burns & Oates.

Rahner, Karl, and Johann Baptist Metz. 1968. *Spirit in the World.* Trans. William V. Dych. New York: Herder and Herder.

Russell, Letty M. 1993. *Church in the Round: Feminist Interpretation of the Church*. 1st ed. Louisville: Westminster/John Knox.

Russell, Letty M. (*et al.*). 2009. *Just Hospitality: God's Welcome in a World of Difference*. 1st ed. Louisville: Westminster/John Knox.

Smith, James K. A. 2009. *Desiring the Kingdom: Worship, Worldview, and Cultural Formation*. Grand Rapids: Baker.

Smith, James K. A. 2016. *You Are What You Love: The Spiritual Power of Habit*. Grand Rapids: Brazos Press.

Teresa of Avila. 2025. *The Interior Castle*. Trans. Kieran Kavanaugh, and Otillo Rodriguez. Mahwah, New Jersey: Paulist Press.

Turner, H. E. W. 1954. *The Pattern of Christian Truth: A Study in the Relations between Orthodoxy and Heresy in the Early Church*. New York: AMS Press.

Volf, Miroslav. 1998. *After Our Likeness: The Church as the Image of the Trinity*. Grand Rapids: Eerdmans.

_____. 2019. *Exclusion & Embrace: A Theological Exploration of Identity, Otherness, and Reconciliation*. Revised and updated edition. Nashville: Abingdon.

_____. 2021. *The End of Memory: Remembering Rightly in a Violent World*. Second edition. Grand Rapids: Eerdmans.

Wainwright, Geoffrey. 1980. *Doxology: The Praise of God in Worship, Doctrine and Life*. Oxford: Oxford University Press.

Wessel, Susan. 2010. "Memory and Individuality in Gregory of Nyssa's Dialogus de Anima et Resurrectione." *Journal of Early Christian Studies* 18 (3): 369–92.

Williams, Thomas, ed. 2025. *Augustine's 'Confessions': A Critical Guide*. Cambridge: Cambridge University Press.

Williams, Rowan. 2016. *Being Disciples: Essentials of the Christian Life*. Grand Rapids: Eerdmans.

_____. 2018. *Christ the Heart of Creation*. London: Continuum.

_____. 2000. *On Christian Theology*. Oxford, UK: Blackwell Publishers.

_____. 2003. *The Dwelling of the Light: Praying with Icons of Christ*. Grand Rapids: Eerdmans.

_____. 2007. *Tokens of Trust: An Introduction to Christian Belief*. Louisville: Westminster/John Knox.

Wright, N. T. 2013. *Christian Origins and the Question of God*, Vol. 4: *Paul and the Faithfulness of God*. Minneapolis: Fortress.

_____. 2007. *Surprised by Hope*. London: SPCK.

Young, Frances M., and Andrew Teal. 2010. *From Nicea to Chalcedon: A Guide to the Literature and Its Background*. Second Edition. Grand Rapids: Baker Academic.

Zizioulas, John D. 1985. *Being as Communion: Studies in Personhood and the Church.* Crestwood, N.Y.: St. Vladimir's Seminary Press.

Zizioulas, John D., and Luke Ben Tallon. 2011. *Eucharistic Communion and the World.* London: Continuum.

Index

* For readers who are confused by the index, the author recommends rereading the book.

www.ingramcontent.com/pod-product-compliance
Lightning Source LLC
La Vergne TN
LVHW022322080426
835508LV00041B/2080